Kissing Breakups Goodbye

Kissing Breakups Goodbye

Every relationship has the potential to last longer than we anticipate!

Dr. Harrison S. Mungal, PhD

FOREWORD By: Dr. Randy and Jill Neilson

To order additional copies of this book, contact:
Xlibris LLC
1-888-795-4274
www.Xlibris.com
Orders@Xlibris.com
539282

CONTENTS

I believe that there is the potential for every relationship to last longer than we anticipate. Every couple has the ability to kiss breakups goodbye and focus on a long lasting relationship.

Special thanks to my wife Kathleen Mungal for all her support in assisting to produce this book. Her love for me has given all the reason why a book like this should be published to support couples in their relationships. Forever in love!!!

Editor: Aisha Hammah
Cover photo designed by: Kevin Panlilio
Contact Author via email: hsmungal@hotmail.com
Web: www.kissingbreakupsgoodbye.ca
Web: www.harrisonandkathleen.com
Web: www.agetoage.ca
Facebook: Harrison Mungal
Twitter: harrisonandkathleen@HKrelationships
LinkedIn: Dr. Harrison Mungal PhD
Youtube: Harrison Mungal

ABOUT THE AUTHOR

Dr. Harrison S. Mungal and his wife Kathleen have been married for 24 years (as of 2014). He and Kathleen have seven (7) beautiful children and a son-in-law he considers a son. He has a seasoned background in his relationship with his wife and children; he is family oriented and believes in investing in what he explains as "the inheritance".

Dr. Mungal and Kathleen are hosts of a local television program sponsored by Horizon Interfaith. He has been a guest speaker at over 27 nations, on several radio stations, television programs, churches, community workshops, seminars and conferences. He has received several awards and recognitions from the local police, mayor, community leaders, managers and directors, and the people he supports. Most of the topic he teaches revolves around relationships, sex, marriage and the family, parenting, substance abuse and additions, leadership/mentorship and mental health.

Dr. Mungal is a member of the Canadian Psychological Association and a Founding member for the Canadian Association of Cognitive and Behavioural Therapies (CACBT-ACTCC). He holds a bachelor degree in Theology, two masters degree (MA, MSW) and a PhD.

FOREWORD

By Dr. Randy Neilson and Jill Neilson

It has been said that, "Love makes the world go around." In fact, everyone longs for relationships where they feel accepted and cared for. When relationships are working well, they are exciting, fulfilling and downright thrilling to be a part of. Even the Bible says that it is not good for people to be alone.

Everyone I have met wants to experience the satisfaction found in a healthy relationship. Unfortunately, the thrill of new love is often lost in the mundane routines of daily life. The passion of newlyweds becomes overcome by the challenges of a growing family and careers.

In society, families are fracturing at an alarming rate and fatherless homes are becoming the norm, leaving a legacy of mistrust and broken relationships behind.

That's where this powerful and practical book comes in. It is nothing short of a field-tested blueprint for identifying relationship pressure points and it provides practical insights for truly successful and satisfying relationships.

This book is not written by an academic theorist but by an active practitioner who speaks from firsthand knowledge about relationship challenges and success. Dr. Harrison Mungal has navigated multiple career paths that have led him to work passionately to endow those who have lost hope in having fulfilling relationships with the skills needed to turn their situations around. Not only does he lead a team of helping professionals, he personally counsels couples and individuals who exhibit broken hearts and shattered trust.

Harrison has refined his relationship skills in the laboratory of his own life with the help of his wife of 23 years, Kathleen, and their 7 children. His practical insights will help you regardless of your situation.

This book presents real-life stories that you can relate to. In some, it might shock you that positive change was even possible. You will find helpful hints that will challenge you to make intentional adjustments in your own personal relationships. New hope will rise within you that it is possible to have long-term, satisfying relationships by "kissing breakups goodbye."

There is too much at stake to settle for the status quo. Your family needs its relationships to be strengthened so that you can leave a legacy of healthy, satisfying, life-long partnerships that will be a pattern for future generations. Your family and friends' relational health could be strongly impacted by the decisions you make today and the guidelines presented in this book will equip you to make healthy ones.

Dr. Randy Neilson

I have known Harrison and Kathleen Mungal since the early 1990's when they were missionaries in Croatia during the war. They migrated there with their 3 young children all under the age of 3 years old at the time. Even through difficult situations, this couple has proven to be solid in their relationship.

You can read about Harrison and Kathleen's life journey in this book. As you read, you will realize that the title, "Kissing Breakups Goodbye," is so befitting. Harrison and Kathleen have a passion to see relationships become healthier. They are convinced that no relationship is too difficult to mend. They help us understand that if we are willing to focus on identifying the causes behind the issues we have, then we can effectively work on the solutions. This couple provides therapeutic counselling and has seen many couples' lives change as a result of the support they have provided.

Harrison addresses several key topics he has found to be problematic in relationships that are struggling. Topics such as

"Emotional Scars," "Emotional Affairs," and "Co-Dependency and Passivity" are just a few that have "hit home" for me. Helpful guidance towards implementing effective solutions can be found under headings such as "Setting the Foundation and The Art of Romance."

In this book, Harrison shares that, "There are no perfect relationships or marriages but the potential for healthy relationships is limitless." He also shares that, "Love is an emotion that does not die, but tends to go to sleep." The concept of love is approached from an angle where couples learn how to keep love awake and work towards a relationship with a bright future despite the difficulties that are bound to arise.

Each relationship has the potential to serve as an example for others to follow. The concept of learning from others and at the same time capturing what is best for each relationship is touched on in the pages that follow. Harrison highlights the value of learning from other relationships and mentors and how this can steer families in the right direction before problems become cancerous and destroy relationships.

You will be able to relate to the real-life stories shared in this book. Some are unimaginable and even quite sorrowful. However, success was achieved in many of these instances. True love is possible, as you will explore with Harrison.

Harrison sought me out to write this foreword because I have been married to Dr. Randy Neilson for 46 years. We have had to make hard choices over the years. In my relationship, I have found, you will win or lose by the way you choose. Many people might not be able to be reached by us, but we hope that through this book, they will be reached.

I have seen Harrison and Kathleen adopt godly suggestions and recommendations made by Randy and me to assist others. Their suitability to support couples to better their relationships is evidenced through their own relationship, lifestyle and family. It gives me great pleasure to present the foreword to this book along with my husband Randy.

Jill Neilson

PREFACE

In this book, I will be discussing some of the issues that arise in relationships, the causes and their effects. I will be sharing about what a healthy relationship should look like and what couples should do to maintain their love for one another. You will learn some principles and tools to keep your relationship strong and kiss breakups goodbye.

The title of this book came to heart after one of our conferences where several questions revolving around relationship breakups were asked. This book is going to enhance your relationships as you understand the principles and concepts that keep a couple together and you learn what brings in a wedge of separation. When I brainstormed the concept for this book, I thought of how easy it is for couples to get entangled into relationships that lack purpose and direction. These relationships make it easy for hearts to get steered in the wrong direction. We all have human needs to fulfill. Some of those needs revolve around the emotions that we experience. The heart that feels it is missing the love it needs seeks it out in other places than the relationship.

Kissing Breakups Goodbye will address some of the causes behind poor choices and discuss how the effects our choices can be devastating to a relationship. It will help couples understand before they make irrational decisions to consider the consequences. Every one of us as human beings has power over our heart. We can come to a place where we are moved not by how we feel but by the decisions that we make. Regardless of who we are, we need to take into consideration the consequences of making choices.

My wife, Kathleen, and I have been travelling around the globe doing marriage seminars and teaching couples and singles about choices in relationships. What will keep a couple in a healthy relationship is the choice to be grounded with joy, future expectations and happiness rather than sadness and sorrow. We also have been teaching about the different aspects of relationships that keep the relationship together when there is already a solid foundation. I hope that this book will be as inspiring to you as it has been to those attending our seminars and counselling sessions.

Most couples, and particularly the men in the relationship, have expressed common concerns revolving around the relationship issues that I will discuss. Many people are searching for that magic potion to create a healthy relationship. They are looking for a quick fix to eliminate issues, especially those that are trending in marriages more so today than in the past. According to what I learned from my parents and grandparents, marriage at one time was considered sacred. Regardless of the issues couples faced, they learned how to work them out. There are advantages and disadvantages to looking at the past and, surely, not all aspects of the past apply to today. However, the reality is that couples who make a covenant to live together should be prepared to face the "bumps on the road" that they will encounter in the different seasons of life and there is great validity in the old notion of "sticking together."

In each seminar I am asked a minimum of 15 questions revolving around relationship issues. Couples, for the most part, want to stay together. They're looking for support and educational tools to assist them with making their relationships better.

Kathleen and I have learned from travelling to several countries that the majority of people want their relationships to work. They want what is best for their spouses. We have also learned that regardless of culture and ethnic backgrounds, people express the same concerns everywhere. With that in mind, we have found that when our emotions are affected it hurts the same. It always starts from the heart. Healing also starts from the heart. Once the heart is beating like it should, the feelings for one's spouse awaken.

Some individuals prefer to stay single to avoid issues they see their friends or parents go through in their relationships. Some have developed the fear of becoming committed and withdraw from their partners once a relationship takes a turn towards commitment. We have had individuals say things like, "I cannot see myself like my dad, with all he had to put up with," or "I saw my mother cry night after night when she found out that my dad was cheating. I don't want to go through that." I hope to communicate throughout this book that pursuing a long-term relationship can be a rewarding, worthwhile and joyful endeavor and should not be feared.

Everyone has a story to tell and whether it is good or bad it is their story and it is real. Needless to say, we have to base our life on what is real to us and what we want out of a relationship.

If we are afraid of becoming committed or attached we need to work on the root cause. When we have an issue with keeping long-term relationships, we need to search ourselves and be real about what is preventing us from moving ahead. We shouldn't just make comments like, "We are going a little too fast", or excuses like, "I am not sure if it is God's will for us to be together," and "pull the plug."

Some major questions we hear time and time again are:

- "Why do men cheat?"
- "Why are men never satisfied?"
- "Why do men look at other women when they are married?"
- "Why is my spouse no longer attracted to me?"
- "Is sex an issue in every relationship?
- "How much sex is too much sex?"
- "What is a man looking for that he is not receiving from his spouse?"
- "Why can't my spouse understand me?"
- "What can we do to create trust in our relationship?"
- "Why does my spouse think I'm cheating?"
- "How do I know if my spouse is cheating?"
- "Why is she not dressing up for me?"
- "Is it better to close the book of our relationship since we don't have much intimate time?"

- Why did the romance disappear?"
- "When will my spouse trust me?"
- "We don't communicate anymore. What happened?"
- "Why are we not moving ahead?"
- "Why are finances such an issue in our relationship?"
- "Our cultures clash. Were we never meant to be together?"
- "He doesn't touch me anymore. What should I do?"
- "How can I prove to my spouse she is the love of my life?"
- "Is there such a thing as a happy relationship?"

These are but a small selection of the questions from couples that we have addressed at various events and sessions. My book will attempt to address many of these.

My goal through this book is to educate men and women about having a mate for life, and what it really takes to make a healthy relationship happen. I believe too many people give up too quickly in marriage and relationships, without looking at the root causes of the issues at hand. Relationships might be as easy to acquire as learning how to walk and talk, however we were not born with a guidebook as to how to make one last. We create a healthy relationship by learning from others around us: family, friends, colleagues and professionals. A perfect relationship guidebook has never been passed down because there is no such thing as a perfect relationship. My book is based on this premise.

The joy experienced from a healthy relationship comes with time. We learn from others and we have the choice to take what we know can work for our relationship. Depending on the status of our relationship, we should "chew the meat and spit out the bones," carefully sifting though all of the advice, suggestions and recommendations given to us. Like rearing a child or learning how to be good a friend, a brother, a sister, a son, or a daughter, we carry principles we learn from different facets of life and gather the skills to become experienced. I look at intimate relationships in the same fashion.

This book will take you on a journey where you will be educated and have fun in the process of discovering what a healthy, realistic relationship is all about. You will learn how the power of commitment and compromise can create a positive future. You will read and discover some real-life stories of how couples have had their breakthroughs come about.

Sometimes our eyes become clouded or even blinded by things we might not want to discover, or things we think are not for us. Sometimes our view is blocked by what we perceive from our friends, our parents, grandparents or other relatives. But every situation is different although the problems might appear the same. The key is looking at it from every angle and working with the view that fits for our own relationship.

Please note that I am aware that there are healthy relationships with couples living as partners or common law. The term "spouse" will be used in this book to refer to a partner in a relationship regardless of marital status or living situation.

Some stories in this book were fabricated or embellished for the purposes of illustration. Permission was given for all the real-life stories in this book to be shared. The goal was to inspire those who might be struggling with relationship issues to embrace the idea of "kissing breakups goodbye."

I can guarantee that everyone who reads this book will gain some insight into enhancing their relationship and will be better poised to take their love for their spouse to another level. Readers will learn how to differentiate between the myriad issues that affect relationships as well as learn some helpful tips to address these. I invite you to explore these pointers and get creative about tailoring the solutions to your own relationship as you enjoy the content enclosed.

BREAKING NEWS

It was in the summer of 2010 that I received a phone call from a close friend of ours confiding in us that he was on the verge of a divorce. It was all a surprise to Kathleen and me since our friend's marital issues had been concealed. We knew there were some minor issues that had been going on for over 10 years, however, everyone had issues in their marriage. Our friends were close to us. We spent lots of summers together with their family. We enjoyed camping trips, road trips, weekends out, holiday gatherings and special events together. Their children were close to ours and so were their other friends.

Kathleen was in tears and my heart was searching for words to say when we received the phone call. It was a very awkward moment and I found myself not knowing how to reply or what to say. You cannot just say, "That's good to know." or, "Are you sure you guys know what you're doing?" As a friend, I could not say, "She was never good for you," or "You deserve better." If I did this, I would be showing favour towards my friend, which would have further complicated the already tense situation since we knew them both. It was one of those moments where silence was the best answer and some time was given to process the information.

> *Some relationships might have more dirt than others. Some even have hard-to-erase stains. Regardless of the extent of the muck, the bottom line is that every relationship has some filth that is in need of being removed.*

The news was especially unexpected considering that 3 months prior, we were on vacation together and there was no mention of any pertinent issues in the relationship. Our friends appeared to be in love as they hugged each other and cuddled together by the beach. There were no signs of hostility, anger, or hatred between them. We sat together and reflected on good times. We discussed our children and the joys of raising them. We shared about our faith, friends, careers and future plans.

Kathleen wanted to call and speak to the wife and I wanted to tell my friend all the reasons why he should reconsider. My friend advised that he did not want any religious support as he felt he had received enough from our other friends. We spent about 2 hours on the phone as I listened to all that my friend had to say. He was crying as he shared his heart with me and he was angry at the same time. He saw himself as a "loser," a terrible father, an inefficient husband and an unfaithful friend.

This couple, like most couples, had worked hard to build a successful future. They struggled together financially, struggled with ups and downs in their employment, struggled along their career paths and struggled with having children. The husband was faced with a rather lengthy period of trying to find the right job and switched employment almost every year for 6 years, while his wife pursued an education at the same time as raising 2 children. The wife completed a degree program and found an excellent full-time job that brought in more income than her husband. Working late hours and committing herself to her boss and the company, she became successful within 2 years. There were many weekends where we were alone with our friend and his children, while his wife was out working. When we were at her home, she was either too tired to join us or would spend most of the time talking about her job and the "great boss" she had. Our friend gave the impression that she preferred to socialize with her work colleagues rather than her good old friends.

According to the husband, his wife came home and told him she no longer wanted to continue in the marriage and would be moving out. He stated that this was shocking to him, although he knew that "things were not going the way they should." He shared with me that they had not engaged in any form of intimacy or sex for over 8 months, and that there had been no communication between each other regarding their love life. My friend expressed that he had been running the home, doing the household chores, cooking every day, making lunches, paying the bills, buying groceries and taking their children to school programs and extracurricular activities. He found himself making a lot of excuses on behalf of his wife to friends to account for her absence. As he now reflected on the situation, he remarked, "I cannot believe that this is happening to me," adding, "I did everything that she liked or that I felt she would appreciate."

Like with most couples we counsel, our friend shared that the issue did not start "yesterday." It had been going for some time and he thought that if he left it alone it would die or disappear. He preferred to avoid any form of confrontation in order to reduce the number of arguments in the home and give the appearance to the children that he and his wife were good parents.

About 2 months prior to this shocking phone call, we had a call from another friend sharing that he and his wife had been separated for about 3 months. This friend shared that his wife's concerns were based on the fact that he was "too career driven." He stated that she had been spending a lot of time with her friends and believed that they were responsible for the decision. Our friend worked 12-hour shifts that involved working nights. His wife felt that his job was not the right career for him although he had been working in the same field for over 15 years. He had given up several promotions on account of her disapproval of his work, however, he continued to work in order to "bring in the dough."

These two were also close friends of ours, married longer than us and were facing issues that had been ongoing. They were more open to talk about their issues, however, they gave the impression that they found it more amusing to talk about them than to work on them. Kathleen and I met this couple prior to getting married and had received plenty of excellent advice from them that we took to heart. Spending time with this couple was great considering that we had lots of laughter, funny moments and this great advice from them at the same time. They had 3 children who were older than ours, yet got along well with ours.

It was unfortunate that this couple could not see a future together after 27 years of marriage. I don't like giving suggestions or recommendations unless requested, neither do I feel I should tell others how to live their lives. As much as we love our friends, we are not married to them and could never know all the intimate details that couples share that lead to separation or divorce. We can give our opinions, however, we must remember our ideas might work for us, but can only work for others if applied right and in the right circumstance. Our friends never sought our advice.

We had another couple that was close to us who was struggling in their marriage. They filed for divorce and felt it was too shameful to share this with us. We found out through other friends. Kathleen and I could see this one coming. However, we kept it to ourselves. There was no stability in the relationship. The couple moved over 5 times in 3 years and my friend changed jobs almost every year. He got involved in a "get-rich-quick scheme" selling household and beauty products, pushing nutritional drinks and taking on risky property investments. He is a very good person, has a great personality, and can give great advice, however, he had difficulty understanding how important it was to have a stable life. With a wife and 3 young children, building a home with stability is very important and this was significantly lacking.

Kathleen and I had other acquaintances who called informing us that they had separated. In total, within 4 years we saw 5 of our friends' marriages dissolve. It was sad and hurtful at the same time.

When Kathleen and I found out from one couple that they had separated, it was like finding out a family member was diagnosed with cancer. It was in the middle of winter when we had planned to have dinner together. This couple had been faithful friends; ones we could count on anytime. We met with them and everything appeared to be okay. I thought to myself that things were working well, only to find out the opposite. We were having a good time eating dinner and talking about everything else under the sun except their marriage. Kathleen knew that things were not working out well in the marriage, however, on their last visit, the wife expressed that she would try to work on the issues that she considered major.

What shocking news it was when my friend said, "I have to tell you and Kathleen something. Please don't get upset." His eyes were full of tears. He was shaking like he was having an anxiety attack and he was sweating profusely. He nervously shared that they had decided to separate. Kathleen and I have learned never to point fingers at others, nor give the impression that we are siding with or showing favour to one person more than the other. We were both in shock and wanted to cry along with my friend as he expressed his grief. We felt emotionally attached and wanted to do something as our first reaction, however, we quickly realized that without their solicitation of our advice, the best we could do was pray and hope for the best.

Although we knew our friends and spent quality time with them individually and together, we didn't know them intimately and the personal issues they were going through except the little they told us. Neither one of them saw the need for marital counselling during the relationship.

This couple eventually requested to meet with us to share some of the issues they had been struggling with over the last 6 years. The husband was cooperative in relating some of the issues he was having in his relationship. The fact that they had 3 children all under the age of 7 was a source of stress. He shared that he was dealing with low self-esteem, was working too much and had a poor sex life as well. These were matters he had difficulty sharing with his wife.

The wife also began sharing the issues she was having. She said her husband had been pushing her to have sex almost daily. He was messy. He watched television and played video games all day when he was at home. He refused to do things like take the dog out or spend time with the children. He was always up at night watching pornography (she had caught him masturbating on several occasions). He ate "like a pig," was developing a lot of health issues, refused to visit her parents, treated her like "garbage," never complimented her or thanked her for her hard work in keeping the house clean or caring for the children. He inconsiderately walked ahead of her while out in public and never held her hand. He refused to spend quality time with her and she could not recall the last time he purchased flowers for her or took her out on a date. As the wife opened up, Kathleen and

I gave her some suggestions. She shared the ideas with her husband, however, he refused to listen.

I look at relationships and marriages as unions that must go through the "washing machine of life" that serves to clean up the "dirt" of the past. Some relationships might have more dirt than others. Some even have hard-to-erase stains. Regardless of the extent of the muck, the bottom line is that every relationship has some filth that is in need of being removed. For those who refuse to address the dirt in their relationship, the dirt eventually becomes evident, and those they associate with end up becoming aware of it.

Seeking the right advice from a professional is never the wrong option. When a couple's relationship goes through the wash, the choice of detergent they use will determine the outcome. Some detergents smell nice, but might not do the job well. Others might not have a good smell but will clean up the clothes very well. Most people in our lives will say nice things to avoid conflict or disagreements, however, behind your back they will say exactly what they think. That approach is like detergent that smells good, but does little or nothing to clean up filth in a relationship. Friends, family and colleagues might all want the best for you as they see you struggling in your relationship, but might not want to take the risk of telling it like it is. An outsider, a good professional or someone who has proven that their detergent works well in their own life will tell it to you like it is and is more likely to suggest what is needed to have a stain-free relationship.

When news of a breakup hits, the effect is devastating and awkward for each of the partners involved as well as for the surrounding community of family and friends. Feelings of sadness and hurt can well up in friends, while feelings of inadequacy and shame often surface in partners who are now faced with failure that they can no longer cover up.

As you have seen from the different scenarios in this chapter, the specific details of the issues faced varied from couple to couple, however, there were some common threads among the pairs. In each case, the problems did not just appear overnight. The partners chose to ignore their problems and not to share them with others (or failed to take them seriously). They masked them from outsiders until things got out of control. The idea is to address issues that arise on a daily basis or at least as regularly as possible to avoid them from becoming so big that one no longer feels that they can do anything about them.

We will be exploring several issues in detail in this book. The most common issues we see in relationships at our clinic are related to cheating, lack of trust, little or no communication, disagreements, abuse, jealousy, gossiping, blaming each other, the perception of inadequate attention, control, negativity, finances, in-laws, family and friends, and past relationships. Regardless of its nature, any issue that arises in a relationship should be addressed immediately at the appropriate place and time.

When a relationship is facing a breakup, it is natural for others to want to give advice, but advice is best when solicited. If one or both partners are not willing to seek help, there is nothing one can do. Even when advice is sought, it is important to note that every couple is different and what works for one might not work for the other. Seeking professional help or help from a person with a proven track-record is always a good idea to try to salvage a broken relationship. A professional has a distance from the relationship that family and friends don't have and is in a better position to tell it like it is.

Points to Ponder:

1. Have you had any close friends or relatives separate recently? What was your reaction?
2. What happens in a relationship when the 2 people involved ignore the issues?
3. Who is the best person to approach for advice in your marriage?

CUT TO THE CHASE

Men and Women Are Not Alike . . .

In society, we often like to say that each individual is uniquely different. While this is true in its own regard, it is also true that some quite accurate generalizations can be made about the wants, perceptions and relational patterns of the sexes. In the majority of our seminars and conferences, when we split the men and the women up and get them to ask questions, we find women always want to know "why all men want sex?" The very question reveals a fundamental difference in understanding between men and women. Most men agree that sex is not a want; it's a *necessity*.

Sex is important, as most men would concur, however, especially within a certain age bracket, what a man is looking for even more than sex is a woman who he knows will draw the attention of others. With that being said, he is not necessarily looking for a woman who is a model, but one who is confident and secure, a woman who has a bright smile, happy demeanor and is not afraid to say what she wants.

The purpose of outside attraction is to serve as an "outward note" that a person exists.

The same behavioural patterns pop up again and again with men in relationships. For instance, most men want what they can't have. I

29

think of King David who had all he could ever want in life. He was a great king. He could have had any woman and marry as many as he desired, yet he sought out Bathsheba, the wife of Uriah. He ended up having Uriah killed as a result of his strong desire for her. There is this strong desire in men to pursue the unattainable. However, since the perfect woman is hard to find, many will spend most of their time trying to "spill their seed" on other ground until the perfect woman comes along.

Men can be very insecure when it comes to the right woman and often have difficulty making their feelings and emotions known. They might need the assistance of the woman to help speed up the process. Then there are men who are very vocal about what they want and some have emotion-suppressing attitudes. Depending on their upbringing and past issues, they can be very dominant and even abusive.

The old-fashioned guy will try to wait until the woman of his dreams enters the scene. During the waiting period, he explores any opportunity that comes along. This is the type of guy who might not get married until his late 30's or later. He lives in fear of committing himself to "the wrong person." He has difficulty seeing beyond the day-to-day issues most couples go through.

The guy who is looking to build a future is hard to discover, as his mind can be easily polluted by what society pushes. We see today that society promotes that a normal relationship might not necessarily mean marriage but can mean living in a common law relationship. In fact, the law now states that if 2 people are living together for a period (3 years, for example) they are considered to be like a married couple. Should they decide to separate they are treated in the same fashion as those who are married and are filing for divorce.

When hope is lost or cannot be seen, a good man might lose touch with reality and often quickly move in with a woman, only to then tie the knot with someone who has come short of his vision.

Men looking for satisfaction outside of their relationships is a common complaint that women in troubled relationships have. Generally speaking, a man wants someone who looks beautiful in his eyes, but also someone that makes his heart come alive and who he considers his best friend. Unfortunately, such a relationship might start off on the right track and then as time passes by, the woman ceases to be his best friend. She becomes like just another friend, a colleague or a peer. The moment a man starts losing the joy of being happy around his spouse, he seeks alternatives to replace the empty feeling without even thinking about it.

So what can make a man feel happy? One area that often comes up is the outward appearance of a woman. Some examples of things many men say they look for are bright eyes, a nice shape, nice-smelling hair, clean nails, a clean body and a nice sense of fashion without too much make-up.

As Kathleen and I have seen from our seminars, most men when prompted will vocalize that once a woman is looking and dressing well, smells good and presents herself in a "womanly fashion," she can win their heart. However, once the couple is married, men complain about the cost of clothes and excessive shopping. Every woman should dress according to her financial status when she is married and use common sense as to what to buy and when to buy it. When we are single we can spend more on ourselves than when we are married. The responsibility of bills can become overwhelming, especially for men in relationships.

I like my wife to look good. She should feel comfortable in what she wears and not necessarily dress for me, but for herself. I fell in love with Kathleen's heart and not her outfit. The typical woman wants to dress to please her man and she loses her inward identity as she tries to look like a model from a magazine. The difference between her and the model in the magazine is the fact that the model in the magazine did not spend $800.00 on one suit or $1200.00 on make-up to look the way she did. Her look was paid for by her employer. We all have our own likes and dislikes and there is no need to change the clothes we wear to please our spouse, but of course, there are the exceptions. A woman should not wear blue jeans to a formal dinner or evening wear to a barbeque. We also need to live in the here and now and show this through modern dress. It is important in a relationship to maintain a style that brings out our identity, shows our personality and reveals our character.

There are subtle details to consider when putting a look together. My wife and I come from 2 different continents and when we were first married, Kathleen would buy me dark clothes and I could not understand why. Soon I realized that the coordination of clothing colour and skin tone can help to complete one's look. Dark clothes typically look much nicer on lighter skin tones than dark tones and so Kathleen was used to buying colours which looked good on her. Some colours bring out the complexion of a person and their internal shine better than others. It is worth considering these elements of dress before the relationship begins and maintaining them throughout.

Though outward appearance comes up a lot, most guys would agree, especially those who are married or looking for a relationship, that the heart of a woman is the focal point. The few guys who are seeking for a perfect-looking woman are only looking for their own image to be boosted.

Relationships that are driven by outward appearance have more issues than those that are focused on falling in love with the heart. Don't get me wrong, we all need to take care of ourselves and look good for our spouse, however, maintaining looks should not be the essence of what we bring to the relationship.

It might be interesting to learn that most men prefer a woman with an average-sized body. Depending on the guy, he might not even really care about the appearance at all. A woman's personality bears more of an importance to most men than just her looks. Self-confidence, independence, kindness, a loveable character, a nice smile and being fun to be around will stir up more of an attraction in a serious man.

Some women are convinced that men are looking for superficial things and end up spending lots of money on the pursuit of a perfect body: the perfect hair, the perfect teeth, the perfect breasts. However, it is the heart of a woman that will draw a man to her. The purpose of outside attraction is to serve as an "outward note" that a person exists. However, it is a woman's heart that will attract the guy with the desire for a long-term relationship.

There are a number of personal attributes that come up on the top of most men's checklists. Men look for a woman who will make every effort she can to please him, someone who can make him look his best, someone who has faith in him, someone who expresses their appreciations for a job well done, someone who gives compliments when needed. A man wants a woman who is not the gossip hippy of the town, but focuses her interest on him, a woman who is not a "nag," one who is not overbearing, one who is warm with a positive attitude.

While guys who are the dominant type might look for a woman they can treat like their doormat, most men look for a woman who will bring some light into their heart. I'll tell you, when I received my birthday gift in October of 2013 from my wife, "101 Reasons Why I Love You," I felt that there were no words to express the feeling of joy I had. Kathleen made a photo book with 101 reasons why she loves me and I felt like a fire was rekindled, another level of love was unveiled, and the words "I love you" had a much greater meaning.

Any woman who endorses a positive attitude can light up the coldest room in a man's heart. A sense of humor and knowing how to be respectful will reveal the hidden quarters of a man's soul. A woman, who is comfortable with her sexuality and not afraid to explore her physical expression of love for her spouse can bring out the best in her husband.

Men are looking for a woman who will make them "feel like a man." The qualities that I have mentioned are some basic ones a woman can start with. These are attributes that can be learned as we were not born with them. Some good mentoring and training in these areas can open a lot of doors for the right man and woman.

The fact that most men are looking for the same things in life never ceases to boggle my mind. Regardless of culture or ethnic background, there is this notion that a man's happiness requires that he be "treated like a man." Though there are the rare exceptions like those who prefer their spouses to be domineering, this is true virtually across the board.

Every man has his own strengths and weaknesses. He deals with his own issues and insecurities, however, when he finds a woman who can appreciate his strengths and weaknesses, it brings him to another level in his life where his confidence rises and his issues and insecurities seem like molehills rather than mountains. A woman's ability to complement a man's qualities, both good and bad, is a form of compatibility between a pair. When we learn to work with each other's differences and to balance out one another, the relationship takes on a new dimension.

Important to our understanding of relationship behaviours. I would like to briefly outline a key factor that shapes men's relationships and then we will look at one for women. When I look at men who were raised in homes where there was a father present, the men follow in their fathers' footsteps. An abusive father sets an example for his son to follow his pattern. A husband who treats his wife without respect and leaves no room for her to find herself, has a son who does the same to his spouse. We are not born with the gift of knowing how to be a man or a woman. The people around us play the very important role of being models in our lives.

I was counselling a man who was afraid of making a commitment with his girlfriend although he loved her and wanted to be with her. He could not see himself taking the next step of allowing her to know how he truly felt. He was afraid that the relationship would turn into a disaster and had a fear of being mistreated by the woman of his dreams as this was the pattern that his past relationships took on. This client was greatly affected by the role his father played in his parents' relationship. His mother wore the pants in the home and was overbearing to say the least, while his father was overly submissive. As a way of diverting his attention from his sorrows, his father worked excessively to the point where he became a workaholic. My client had resolved that he never wanted to be like his father yet judging by his past, he indeed was.

This is not to say that a man cannot change the negative patterns in his life shaped by his father figure. Our client had a friend who on the other hand was a great example of an assertive yet giving spouse. He would buy flowers for his wife on a regular basis, give her gifts and take her out regularly, but he still was able to maintain his role as the head of the house. My client was able to use his friend as an example to model after, which helped him to focus on a positive example as he moved ahead in his own relationship.

In the case of a lot of women, the way they respond in relationships often surrounds their feelings about beauty, self-image and how others see them. This is tightly linked to feelings of self-worth. Men might look at other men to compare their body types.

They might think, *Why is she with that loser?* or *How can a guy like that have such a beautiful woman?* Beyond that, men don't really compare themselves like women do. Women compare their clothes, hair, make-up and bodies, and often rate themselves too modestly. How about the mounds of money women spend on clothes they'll probably never wear again to impress others? Women live in a world that is driven by the pressure to keep up a perfect image.

Women are pressured to fit a certain mold in the world of fashion and beauty. Most department stores are geared towards women. There is a greater variety of clothes and accessories for women than for children or men. Some women become under-confident and insecure, as they are unable to keep up with society's expectations.

It turns out that how a woman interacts with a partner tends to be a reflection her self-image rather than the presence of a specific role model as in the case of men. What happens is when some women feel like they don't measure up, they end up not caring for themselves. They are no longer driven to maintain their body image or maintain relationships with friends who do. This then affects their dating life. This happens for 2 main reasons. One is that men are drawn to women with confidence. The other is that when a woman doesn't feel confident, she might be more inclined to shy away from relationships or sabotage the ones she has.

Other women prefer to stay at home and live lives revolving around those they feel they can trust the most. Their spouse and children become their world. If they are single, they might sleep around with guys who show an interest in them with hopes that the man will make them feel special and become committed. When this doesn't happen it drives them even further away from the world.

Other women, still, might become focused on the one thing that gives them hope: that is the church. This can become dangerous only if the woman closes herself off to everything else, including professional counsel and the suggestions of those closest to her.

The media has portrayed a beautiful female to be busty with a perfect body, skinny with a few pieces of clothes on and flawless skin that looks as soft as a "baby's bottom." The message the media delivers is, "This is every man's dream!" NOT!!! You have probably discovered by now, men think differently.

We can all agree that women think differently than men and that a woman's needs and desires are different from men's. We should never pretend that we can understand each other without taking time to study one another. Until we take the time to understand each sex, male and female, we cannot move on to appreciate fully, the uniqueness of each other.

Points to Ponder:

1. Is sex a need or a want for men?
2. How can a woman touch a man's heart?
3. Why is it important for a man to treat a woman with respect in the home?
4. What are some important considerations for physical appearance and why is physical appearance important?
5. What are some ways men differ from women in their needs, desires and behaviours?

THE PARKING LOT ISSUE

It was a beautiful spring morning. It was a Sunday. We pulled into the church parking lot ready for the coming service. The children were all in a good mood. They had been singing during the drive down and talking about how they were looking forward to worshiping with our church family. As we parked the car, we heard yelling and swearing in the parking lot. I thought to myself, *There must be a domestic dispute about to take plac*e. I scanned the parking lot and then saw a couple with 2 children briskly walking towards the church. There was no one else around. They had just been verbally abusive to each other. Our children were very surprised by what they were witnessing in the parking lot of the church. I reminded them that the church is made of all types of people with different lifestyles.

During the church service, I turned to look around while everyone was standing and singing and I observed the husband sitting with his chest bent over towards his knees. He was shaking like a leaf. His spouse was singing and worshiping along with their children as though nothing had happened. I sat through that service trying to process what might have gone wrong. For the couple to argue like that on the church grounds, there were definitely some issues there that had been festering for some time.

> *The nature of mankind is to look at others and point out their flaws. Unless we psychologically train our minds to focus on the positive aspects of others, we are bound to do this to our spouses because they will undoubtedly come with flaws.*

That day our children said to Kathleen and me that they appreciated the fact that we never argued in public or in front of them. I saw that our choice as a couple not to argue in front of our children caused our children to respect us even more at a moment like that when their eyes were opened to the reality of the discord that some other couples live with.

Although we all have issues in our marriages, we should never allow our children to be a part of them. Children should never have to take on the responsibility of having to choose sides between parents. I see how children's minds are corrupted as parents influence them by creating an atmosphere where they must choose their father over their mother or vice versa. We create hatred towards the opposite sex in our children when we express the perception that our spouse is wrong in their presence.

So how does a couple get to the point that they will argue abusively, oblivious to their surroundings? Kathleen and I encourage couples to separate the issue from the spouse. When an individual is focused on their spouse instead of on the issues at hand, it is much easier for them to get carried away in a disagreement.

It is important to note that there are a number of sources of issues in relationships. Some couples might deal with unresolved abuse from the past. This could be verbal, physical, sexual or emotional abuse.

Some couples might struggle with substance abuse, other addictions, poor mental or physical health, identity issues, anger issues, time management issues or poor self-esteem. The list goes on and these days, it's natural for each partner to come into a relationship with a number of these factors to deal with. These are not small issues one can just ignore or avoid and expect to disappear.

Then there are the issues that arise from the fact that each person in a couple is a unique individual with unique exposures and preferences. When Kathleen and I got married, there were definitely some issues. We had problems revolving around our different upbringings, cultural differences, ethnic acceptance, the way grocery shopping was done, the type of food we ate, the type of people we hung around with, the way we decorated our home, the type of clothing we wore, the way money was budgeted, and the list goes on and on.

I must elaborate here on issues surrounding sex outside of marriage. This is a big one. Today what we see is that a lot of people are having sex with or without their spouses to avoid life's issues. Sex is being used as a form of venting. The flesh has a mind of its own and craves intimacy to bring about feelings of self-worth. Godly morals are compromised and the boundaries that have been established even from childhood get crossed.

Kathleen's love for me has kept me on track from indulging in my own fantasies. We have to understand that although sex is something good and created by God, it should happen only with the person you decide to love for the rest of your life. Scarring your sexual life by illegitimate sex can cause serious issues in long-term relationships.

The nature of mankind is to look at others and point out their flaws. Unless we psychologically train our minds to focus on the positive aspects of others, we are bound to do this to our spouses because they will undoubtedly come with flaws. Pointing fingers at others makes us feel good about ourselves. However, our own issues build up and we erupt like volcanoes sooner or later. At the same time, we are looking in the wrong place so we are not positioned at a place where we can start focusing on solutions.

Today, Kathleen and I have matured in handling issues. This is one reason why I felt confident in writing this book. We have learned to try our best never to allow issues to attach themselves to us personally and it has worked well. There is nothing that should be able to cause a couple to lose sight of the love they have for one another under it all.

Part of me felt obligated to address the issue in the parking lot we witnessed. However, the other part of me felt I shouldn't get involved. I did purpose in my heart to address the issue if I ever saw it happening again. Since most people in our church are aware of our clinic, I expected that this couple would contact us for an appointment if they felt it was needed.

One lesson from the parking lot story is we need to choose the right time and place to address relationship issues with our spouse. Yelling and swearing in public or in front of the children does not bring solutions. I suggest for couples to go out for dinner to have discussions that might be potentially heavy. In such a setting there is an awareness of others around you and the chances are you will keep your volume low. Your spouse, in turn, will more effectively hear what you have to say.

A rule of thumb to remember is that an issue cannot be resolved by opinions or an overly expressive tone of voice. These are indicators that you are probably focusing on the person and not the real issues. It is much more fruitful to address the facts of the issue. When we separate the issue from the person, we soon realize how minor it is and it is easier to work at it. Solutions come faster this way as it is always much simpler to resolve an issue than to change a person.

Points to Ponder:

1. What does arguing in front of your children tell them about your relationship?
2. What types of things can happen when issues are not dealt with in a relationship?
3. Where should relationship issues be discussed?

THE FRUIT TREE

All relationships between 2 spouses can be likened to a fruit tree. The more it is watered and taken care of, the faster it can grow and bring forth beautiful fruit.

I see the man in a relationship to be like the root of a tree. The root brings in all the necessary nutrients required for the plant to survive. It is the man's responsibility to make sure the relationship has sufficient "food" such as shelter, stability, guidelines, structure, protection, discipline, spiritual grounding, godly morals and financial support among other things. He facilitates the process of finding food by his very nature.

The roots also act as a protector for the plant and the man is the protector for his family. He will help the family to stand strong and firm by doing everything in his power to nourish the tree of the relationship. If he dishonours his spouse, he invites an infection in the relationship that can eventually cause the relationship to shrivel and die.

Just as the importance of the roots to the tree as a whole cannot be downplayed, the importance of a person's unique responsibility in the family unit ought not to be downplayed.

A stem grows as long as the roots are providing the right food. The woman in the relationship is like the stem of a plant. She is attached to the root. The stronger the roots, the healthier the stem is.

The man and woman in a relationship are connected in a very special way. If the stem of the tree gets infected with disease, the roots of the plant eventually die. If a woman allows herself to be infected by the things of the world or the persuasion of others, she infects the relationship and can cause the root of the plant to die. Infections can spread like a cancer and kill a relationship.

If the root system is not strong in a relationship, when the wind blows the stem will be broken or destroyed more easily. I see women falling apart when they cannot trust their spouse or depend on him for support. We often say women are driven by emotions. I believe their emotions get caught up in the situations of life which can create issues.

If the "winds of life" are blowing the stem, the roots might feel the pressure more so than the stem. If a woman is at home, she has the children to care for, the household chores to do, her husband to support, the extended family to entertain, events and gatherings to plan, the neighbours and friends to socialize with, as well as her spiritual life to juggle. If she has a career outside of the home, she has to do double the work. Since the majority of women take it upon themselves to be social butterflies and to care for those around them, like an exposed stem, there are so many potential areas of additional stress if things are not balanced effectively.

Beautiful, sweet, succulent, aromatic, nutrient-rich and plentiful fruit are the results of a healthy fruit tree. When women are supported in all the areas of their life, their relationship will be healthy and happy. They will feel the urge to bear fruits. Although some women might have children for the wrong reasons, most women entertain thoughts of having children when they feel safe, comfortable and stable in a relationship.

Some of the more obvious fruits of a relationship are the children that result. Children can be healthy once the roots continue to maintain nourishment and stability. Unfortunately, in single-parent families, the primary parent carries the weight of having to act as both the root system and the stem to maintain the health of the fruit.

We have learned through counselling that single parents face more challenges managing the family than couples do. Some single parents find it very difficult to sustain the role of having to function as 2 parents. They might appear like any other tree, however, can be underdeveloped, infested or have a compromised root system. Some can easily bend or break when the winds of life come, yet, some have been able to flourish with the support of family members, friends and their community.

Although many single parents have been able to raise children that are family-oriented and kind-hearted, children who are raised by both parents have the benefits of 2 worlds, especially if their parents invest in spending time with them.

As the male figure in the home, I took the responsibility of making sure the family was financially secure. It was a choice I made to walk into maturity as a man and construct a life of stability for my family. Today, the widespread tolerance of men who have too much free-time on their hands or who don't take their responsibility as the provider seriously has created several issues for couples. Some common issues that arise are men getting involved with drugs and alcohol, gambling and other addictions, pornography, infidelity, medical issues from overeating, psychological issues from developing low self-esteem and a whole barrage of related mental health issues. Just as the importance of the roots to the tree as a whole cannot be downplayed, the importance of a person's unique responsibility in the family unit ought not to be downplayed.

I remember working 3 jobs, sometimes 4, to make ends meet. I would work around the clock at times. I fell asleep on a few occasions driving home as I could hardly stay awake. I knew I had to maintain an income to pay the rent and put food on the table. I remember one occasion in particular while driving home. I dozed off at the wheel and swerved off the road and into a ditch. This event was so frustrating that I became very angry at God for allowing it to happen. However, the point is we must do whatever needs to be done in the role we play in a relationship.

I developed my roots by pursuing all that I felt needed to be done at different times in the relationship. The children were always dressed in clean clothes, ate well and showed good manners. We had a very balanced spiritual life, family life, social life, physical life and educational life. These can be seen as fruit as well.

I like to think that trails, mistakes and the wrong decisions we experience are like dung. Dung smells and it's dirty. No one wants to stand around and enjoy its aroma. However, dung is used as a fertilizer for plants to bring forth a healthy harvest. Our past struggles can do the same to help fertilize a healthy and fruitful relationship.

As a couple we have done church planting, pastoring, missions, public-speaking and started our own business. Each of these endeavors came with its own trials as we tried to provide for our children. At times we shopped at thrift stores and took used clothing from family and friends. Kathleen would buy items with reduced prices at the grocery store. No one knew the struggles we were going through and no one showed that they were interested in knowing about our lives. We kept our faith and focused on the family.

Then, I started to travel once or twice a month to speak at churches and seminars, leaving Kathleen at home with the children. Kathleen managed a small retail business while homeschooling the children.

When I look back at our past, there are many things I wish I could have changed so that I could have spent more time with my family. I wish I had a mentor or guide to assist with making decisions. There were many mistakes made which I probably would not repeat today if I had the chance to do things over again. Kathleen and I have learned from these untoward experiences and this has made our relationship stronger.

An added benefit was that when our children saw the struggles we went through to create a stable home they seemed to appreciate what they did have more so than children who got whatever they wanted. The children would hear me singing with joy, regardless of our financial status. They would hear us praying in the basement. We prayed as a family to address the needs and celebrated as the answers came. We have never really had to endure the stresses of, "Dad, I want this," or "Dad, I want that" because our children were happy and content with whatever they got (and still are). None of our children complained about not having what other children had. They never compared themselves with other children. Some of our older children remember what we went through and have nurtured the younger children.

Kathleen did what she had to do to keep the family alive, and I did what I needed to do to keep our marriage alive. Our main pillars were God and the love we had for each other.

Today, I see how our past has brought our relationship to another dimension. Our love has grown so strong it is difficult to put it in words. It is like our hearts have truly become one. We have developed a strong family with healthy traditions and a close bond. The love between Kathleen and me and the character displayed in our children reflect the picture of a well-nourished fruit tree.

It takes 2 to create a life that can either bring happiness or sadness, but the two are of one organism. I hope that you and your spouse will be encouraged to create happiness as a unit and bear lots of fruit.

Points to Ponder:

1. If a fruit tree is used as an illustration where the man is the root system of the tree, what does that role require of him?
2. What is the woman's part to play in the fruit tree analogy?
3. How do the problems of our past and present help our children?
4. What type of fruit does your relationship produce?

EMOTIONAL SCARS

As we conceptualize relationships, we cannot ignore the engine that keeps relationships alive. Our relationships are driven by emotions and emotions often drive our relationships. Emotions are our response to something good or bad that comes across our path. Emotions are like the skin to the soul. They feel and the feelings can be positive or negative.

Unfortunately, many people carry negative feelings from bad things they have experienced in the past. They have difficulty letting go of past experiences and this hinders the healing of the emotional scar that was created. It is not the traumatic event itself that affects the person, but the feeling

The consequences of the "whatever feels good, do it" mentality leaves scar on one's emotions that can cripple a relationship.

of the experience that causes the scar, which is why we call them "emotional scars." A scar can often give the illusion that a wound has healed though it has not and many people enter relationships with emotional scars they think have already fully healed.

The bigger the wound, the larger the scar is. For some people emotional scars are so big they have difficulty getting used to it and they carry it throughout their lives. For others, they have come to the point where they realize that they have a scar. They might see the scar, admit they have it, but fail to reflect on the cause of the scar.

When we look at the media today, there is a pressure pushing at the hearts of children at a much younger age than when I was growing up. Some of the messages and ideas the media pushes are you have to look flawless, you have to have a sex life, and you can create your own moral standards. Children are having sex in their early teen years. We see a higher rate of teen pregnancy, plus abortions, identity issues, problems with body image and with sexuality and a number of other issues stemming from this form of influence. Children are growing up with a mentality that if something makes them feel good, they should "just do it." Adults are quickly adapting to this new norm and this is causing more and more psychological issues in society.

There are so many children struggling with emotional scars that are the consequence of negative media influences. Some scars are so unbearable that suicide seems to be the only solution for these young people. As these children move on into adulthood, they have their past to deal with which many times becomes a roadblock. Adults who follow what the media promotes are affected in the same way.

The choices we make can affect our mental health and leave long-term scars. Sex is a good example. More and more people are exploring their fantasies and looking for opportunities to fulfill them. I have had so many men between the ages of 35 and 55 say something to the effect of, "I want to try something new although it seems silly." People's fantasies are causing them to develop habits which eventually become addictions. In the past, people did not give a second thought to exploring sexuality to the extent to which it is being explored today. People learned to get rid of thoughts that did not align with good morals. However, today, "everything goes" and this is reflected in the explosion of addictive behaviours that we presently see.

I have had to help men deal with issues surrounding affairs, orgies, swinger's clubs, same sex encounters, pornography and other related issues that affected their marriage. Some of these individuals have shared that they felt like committing suicide because they could not bear the immense pain of the guilt they felt.

The consequences of the "whatever feels good, do it" mentality leaves scar on one's emotions that can cripple a relationship. When the bad habit becomes an addiction, the scars become deeper and can be difficult to treat. The scars affect the emotional well-being of the person afflicted, creating psychological issues. Their relationships suffer as a result.

I have had men and women who cheated on their spouses as they chose to live out their fantasies. These clients express how sorry they are for making the wrong choice and attempting to fulfill their lusts. Their fantasies turned sour when they led to unforeseen consequences such as sexual assault by a sex partner or stress from the unnecessary drama that comes with being with multiple partners. Some ended up taking street drugs to treat their emotional pain and ended up with addiction issues.

Imagine being emotionally scarred from your past choices, finding someone who really cares for you and having to live with the pain of the guilt every day. Some people can hold it together for a while, however, when the usual pressures of life arise, they crack.

It's not just the choices we make in life that can scar us emotionally. I have learned that people's emotions can be affected by a variety of circumstances outside of their control. Emotional scars can arise from breakups, a significant relationship that went wrong, bullying, humiliation, a life-threatening illness, a disability, an automobile accident, sexual dysfunction and many other sources.

A person's emotional being can be scarred unexpectedly. Psychological trauma can result from rape, incest, molestation, domestic abuse, serious bodily harm, witnessing a horrifying injury or a fatality.

In addition circumstances surrounding family life such as children witnessing their parents physically or verbally abuse one another, divorce and moving from one location to another can contribute to emotional scarring.

Some people have developed scars from vicarious or secondary trauma. Seeing parents and other loved ones suffering with depression, anxiety, psychosis, addictions or substance abuse also needs to be taken into consideration when exploring the emotional realm of a person.

Hearing about a negative circumstance in another person's life can affect the emotions of a person. How many of us have become sad for those who are struggling with a medical issue or a mental health issue?

Emotional trauma can last a decade or more in the life of a person. Those who have been sexually abused, or verbally or physically assaulted can have flashbacks and this takes time to cure.

Some signs that one's emotional being is compromised are eating too much, not eating enough and disruptive or unusual sleep patterns that are unusual for the person. Sexual dysfunction, low energy and chronic or unexplained pain also indicate that a person needs to be assessed. Someone who is feeling depressed for no apparent reason, crying uncontrollably, feeling helpless, restless or hopeless might also fall into this category. One who is experiencing anxiety, panic attacks or fear, or who is exhibiting obsessive-compulsive behaviour is also suspect. People with unresolved emotional trauma often express feeling "loss of control," "irritable," "emotionally numb," "resentful" or "angry." They often express that they are unable to carry out their daily routines effectively.

I have clients who have memory lapses, have difficulty making simple decisions, are unable to concentrate and show other symptoms of ADHD. Some clients have developed emotional numbness where nothing fazes them, while others avoid even the mention of topics that bring up the past. The latter will avoid any situation that resembles the event that took place in their life that left the scar. They express feeling depressed, hyper-vigilant, jumpy, detached, overly defensive and often overreact.

When these signs are present, psychological support is necessary. A person with unhealed emotional scars might become ruled by impulsive behaviour, lose the ability to make rational decisions or have difficulty controlling their thoughts.

Like every wound, there is always the possibility that healing can take place. Over time, our emotional scars can heal fully, often with the help of professional therapy. Sometimes the symptoms don't go away or might appear to be gone only to resurface again under a stressful situation. However, it is always worth a try. Anyone who is struggling with emotional scars should seek out support. Just as much as the physical body that is hurt needs healing, the emotional being that is hurt needs healing. In fact. the emotional being takes longer to heal than the physical body so special care must be taken.

Emotional scars can last forever. however. the underlying pain can be eliminated. As I thought about this subject. I was reminded of an incident that took place when I was about 5 years old.

As a young child. I spent most of my time at my maternal grandmother's home. One day I was at my grandma's house while my mother was out shopping. I noticed that the water jug in the fridge was empty and decided to fill it from the tap. The problem was that the tap was downstairs and the jug was made of glass. When I was 4 steps away from the bottom of the stairs. my foot got caught on the step and I fell on top of the glass jug. It shattered into many pieces. one that embedded itself deep into my chest. It was a large piece. measuring at least 3 inches by 4 inches.

The large piece of glass pierced the left side of my chest. punctured my left lung and stopped a pinpoint's diameter away from my heart. The glass could not be seen from the outside. so no one knew how big the piece was. Blood was squirting out everywhere and I lost consciousness. I was rushed to the hospital and ended up on the operation table after-hours.

Eventually. the doctors were able to remove the piece of glass and sew me up. About 1 month later. I came home. My chest had 3 large scars and there were others. I had restrictions on playing sports and my mother watched me like a hawk. I felt embarrassed about the scars and refused to swim or go anywhere without a t-shirt in spite of the hot climate. I would avoid going to the gym or the boys' changeroom so no one could see my chest. I struggled over my body image for over 27 years because of this incident. I lived with a fear of the negative things others might say about my chest or the questions they would ask which I was not prepared to answer. Eventually. I became comfortable with myself. As I opened up, others were able to see my scars which forced me to be prepared to answer questions and talk about what caused them. I had to face my fears, stop blaming myself and focus on emotional healing. In the end. I felt more secure living in the reality of what had happened to me rather than fuelling my fears about what people might think of me.

This incident resulted in emotional scarring that took decades to be resolved. I use this story to highlight the path to healing. Scars don't heal completely unless they are recognized and dealt with. At the same time, their conspicuous nature presents an opportunity for the issues that created them to pop up again and again as we interact with others who notice them.

When we get a wound, we dress it and protect it with a covering in order to stimulate healing. Only those who face their fears and accept their emotional scars move ahead. Although the scar remains as a reminder of the incident that happened, you can learn how to live with it and move on.

Many walk into relationships with emotional scars that haven't fully healed. Emotional scars become relationship problems when couples allow their feelings from past hurts to run their relationships. It is best that unhealed emotional scars be addressed because a healthy relationship requires both individuals to be in a place where they can give the best of themselves.

We cannot change the past, but we can change the future. We learn from the past to better the future. I always tell our children once the jug is broken, we cannot fix it. The key is prevention. There will always be the possibility of being scarred in life. If it happens, we must resolve to get over the trauma and work on finding permanent healing.

Points to Ponder:

1. How does the "whatever feels good, do it" notion affect our generation today?
2. What does it mean to be emotionally scarred?
3. What are some "signs" that someone's emotional being is compromised?
4. What happens when an emotional scar is ignored?
5. What is common in relationships affected by emotional scars?

SHE SHARED HER STORY

I had a client who had been married for over 24 years and who had difficulty letting go of a time in her live when she was 16 years old that greatly upset her emotional well-being. This client migrated to Canada to live with her aunt who promised her a life of happiness. The client had hopes that she would one day bring her parents to live in Canada along with her mother's sister and her family. It was her dream to become a doctor so she could set a good example for her younger siblings.

The client explained that she was happy. The first few weeks she felt like she was in a "land filled with milk and honey." She got a part-time job and was enrolled at a high school. She spoke to her parents every other day and shared how happy she was with the decision to come to Canada.

If we are willing to learn the skills required for our choice of career, we should be willing to invest what is needed to become whole in our relationships as our relationships will greatly affect how we cope in the different stages of life.

One day after school, she stayed behind along with her friends to work on a project where they assisted the teacher. A lot was accomplished and everyone was happy as they spent over 3 hours on the project. The parents of the 3 other friends came by to pick up their daughters and she was left alone. Her ride did not show up and after calling her cousin, he advised that he was running late. Her cousin was a 25-year-old who would bring her to school and pick her up.

On this day her cousin was running late and told her to wait or get a ride with someone else. She decided to wait. However, there was no one around and she began to feel very unsafe. The teacher was leaving the parking lot and saw her waiting. He asked if she wanted a ride home. She decided to take him up on the offer and went with the teacher. On their way home, the teacher took an alternative route, stating it was a shorter way to her house. This young lady, being naïve and new to Canada, did not question the teacher. She respected him as her professor and trusted him.

Unfortunately, the roads led to a secluded area and as she questioned her whereabouts, he stopped the car and sexually assaulted her. The teacher told the client if she told anyone, he would do whatever it took to send her back to her home country. He added that he would fail her in all the courses he taught, she would not be able to graduate or go to university and she would never have a future in Canada.

She went home and showered. She descriptively shared with me how filthy she felt. She was in pain and her mind could not stop replaying the incident that had happened to her. She stated that she felt like she wanted to die, especially when she pictured her teacher all over her. She wanted to rip the skin off of every part of her body that he had touched.

Her cousin called to know her whereabouts and she stated that she was at home. He could hear that she was upset on the phone and decided to come home. His parents were tied up at work and his sister had a night class. Her cousin came home and found her in her room crying. He knew that something was wrong and asked what had happened. She was scared and did not want to say much. He suggested going out for coffee, which she did not feel like doing, however, she agreed.

The client was in her pyjamas and told her cousin that she needed to get dressed. As she was leaving to the bathroom with her clothes, her cousin asked if she had ever had sex with a man. She was shocked at his question and ignored him. He started to laugh and make jokes and he told her that she looked good in her pyjamas. She stated that she was not in the mood for jokes and that she found her cousin to be acting unusual. Little did she know that her cousin had been smoking marijuana with his friends, which was why he didn't pick her up from school.

Her cousin grabbed her and sexually assaulted her. In the moment, she said it felt like she was reliving what had just happened to her just a little over an hour ago with her teacher. Her cousin told her that if she told anyone, he would ask his parents to send her back to her homeland. She came from a well-respected family and their dream was to live in Canada. Their plan was to have her residency in Canada established and then she would sponsor them.

She stated that her cousin left her crying and devastated. She yearned for some support. She looked for a means of killing herself and could not find anything. She wanted to call her parents and take the first fight back to her country. She wanted to run away. She wanted to call her aunt and uncle but was not sure what to say to them. She went to the shower and sat for over an hour crying and not knowing what to do.

The aunt and uncle came home about 2 hours later. She pretended to be fast asleep as she was not sure how she could face them and what she would tell them. She stayed awake for practically the entire night, trying to find some way to get rid of her memory of what had happened to her. She shared how it was like a movie or some tall tale one would read in a book of fiction.

The next day, she woke up and told her aunt that she was not feeling well and would be staying home. The aunt advised that she was heading off to work, however, her husband would be staying home as he was also not feeling well and had a late night. She went to her room and was exhausted, especially since she was up all night trying to process what had happened to her.

Her aunt went to work and both of her cousins went to school. She reported that eventually she was able to calm her thoughts from racing and was able to fall asleep. She described the feeling of exhaustion she had. She felt like a wet towel that someone had wrung to the point that there was no more water left in it. She felt that she had no more life in her and was completely drained of energy. While she was sound asleep, she felt someone in her bed and, to her surprise, it was her uncle. He was naked and forced himself on her, proceeding to sexually assault her.

After this third incident, she was sure that she wanted to die. She could not believe that this was happening to her for the third time within 24 hours. She was told by her uncle that he would send her back to her country and she would never be able to return back to Canada if she told anyone.

She was continually raped for a period of 3 months when she eventually was able to save up enough money to go back to her homeland. She never told her aunt what had happened or reported the teacher. She suffered the trauma of being raped along with having no support to deal with the emotional wounds that were causing her pain. She put up a "psychological wall" in her memory to block out what had happened.

The first 2 years of coping were a disaster as she could not function properly. Her parents thought she was missing Canada and the life she experienced. Although they questioned her as to why she returned home, she never told them what had happened. She made excuses like she was doing poorly at school and felt that she was an inconvenience to her aunt and uncle. She assured them that she would return back to Canada when she was 18 years old.

She was 23 years old when she married the love of her life. She completed her studies as a doctor and graduated with honours as a family physician. Her husband also graduated with honours as a cardiologist. Together they had 3 children: 2 boys and a girl. The entire family moved to Canada and she and her spouse were able to have their certifications transferred to the Canadian standard. She ran a private practice at a walk-in clinic and her husband worked at a hospital. She advised that although from time to time she was able to refocus her thoughts, when she would struggle she would completely "shut down."

During this period in her life, she went through depression and was on anti-depressant medications for years. Whenever she would have overwhelming stressors present, she would fall into "a hole of depression" rethinking what had happened to her at 16 years old. She avoided her uncle and cousin on as many occasions as possible. She made every excuse possible to avoid being in their presence. She never told her husband or her aunt what had happened to her.

Eventually, she sponsored her parents to come to Canada. They lived with her and helped her with her children. She fell into a deep depression as she found herself having to engage with her aunt and uncle more. Her parents enjoyed their company and wanted to spend time with them, especially since she had no other family living in Canada.

One day, her uncle walked into the same room with her and no one else was around. He made a comment about the past and she "lost it." She told him everything she felt inside and how wrong it was for him to have taken advantage of her when she was 16 years old. Everyone could hear her speaking with a higher tone of voice and everyone began listening to the conversation. Her cousin walked into the room and he was also addressed.

Like a volcano, she erupted, and related everything that had happened right there and then. She said everything that had been in her heart for the past 18 years. Everyone was in shock: her parents, her aunts, her husband, her children, her uncle, her cousin who had raped her and his wife and children.

Everyone was upset. Some were speechless as there was no hint that this had taken place. She left that night with her family in a state of brokenness.

She ended up starting the process of therapy that day by exposing the wound that had been infected for over 18 years. There was a build-up of "emotional pus" created by the psychological immune system waiting to be released.

Emotional healing starts when a person is able to talk about their hurts and face the source of the emotional pain. My client needed to work on facing the circumstances that were the source of the deep hurt she was feeling. As she did, her husband better understood why their sex life had not been the greatest.

She had been experiencing nightmares during sex with her husband, but never explained what had happened to her. Her husband suspected sexual assault, however, never explored it.

Eventually, her uncle and aunt received marriage counselling as well as her cousin and his wife. My client is now doing well in her practice and her relationship with her husband has reached another level of love and sexual fulfillment.

Some people have allowed fear from past experiences to conquer them and stop them from moving ahead or effectively cultivating the seed of commitment. Some have become bitter, jaded and closed. They have created walls in their lives as they are afraid to face what else comes along their path. We need to take life as it comes and adapt to every bump and curve that we encounter on life's journey.

There are so many changes and stages we will face in life like falling in love, entering marriage, bearing children, raising children, getting older and experiencing grandparenthood. If we are willing to learn the skills required for our choice of career, we should be willing to invest what is needed to become whole in our relationships as our relationships will greatly affect how we cope in the different stages of life. When we are willing to learn and grow, we will not see failure.

Sometimes you might feel powerless, which leads to anger. This anger might become a good thing, if channelled in the right direction. This anger can become your centre of strength in saying, "Enough is enough. I must rise above my fears."

Points to Ponder:

1. How can fear stop you from moving ahead?
2. How might the ending of the story presented in this chapter influence your attitudes towards your relationship?
3. What are some bumps or curves that have come along your path that you are dealing with today?
4. How can we view our traumatic experiences in a positive way?

IN LOVE WITH LUST

Lust is powerful and also dangerous. For some men, if not most, when they allow testosterone to run their life, it is like red-hot feelings of lust surge wildly in their brains. They become in love with lust and their blood begins to boil on account of hot, lustful feelings. Every girl that passes by becomes an object to be analyzed from head to toe.

Men are prone to fantasizing and recording sexual images in their mind, so that in their alone time they can play the images back stimulate themselves. This is one of the main reasons why pornography is so popular today. Many men, and more and more women, are choosing to watch others having sex and this turns on the pleasure compartment

When it is fulfilled, lust pushes one's boundaries further and further.

of the mind. It stimulates the brain, and individuals and couples consequentially become sexually active. The sex might not be for love, but for lust.

A man has the capacity to easily engage in sex before he forges an emotional bond with a woman. The feelings of pleasure have fooled many men into believing that they are in love with the person when in reality they are in love with the sex. This falls into the category of lust.

One danger that arises with lust is that it can rob a man of his natural strength and his defenses. A woman can have him begging on the floor like a little puppy if she is able to touch the deepest part of his soul through sex. Some women take advantage of this and start premature conversations about marriage or even propose marriage only to see that that the marriage lasts for a short period.

Kathleen and I have dealt with several couples where either the man or the woman believes that they are attracted to someone of the opposite sex or of the same sex other than their spouse. They vocally express the desire to "live in both worlds." They want their marriage to work, but are unwilling to give up their feelings for someone else. Lust will capture the heart of a person and bind him or her to the stimulation that it brings to the detriment of sound rationale.

Lust causes men to think with their bodies rather than their hearts and renders them open to tossing all reason and logic to the wind. We have had clients who reach a point where they are unwilling to look for things they have in common with their spouses, which is an activity we try to encourage when counselling. They no longer want to make attempts to grow in their relationship, nor do they engage in disagreements. They no longer care about their spouse's ins and outs either way.

Though they often appear the same on the surface, lust and love are very different. Lust is the evil twin brother of love. Lust has no feelings, no emotional bonds and makes no commitments. It takes excessive risks and it is willing to sacrifice family, friends, employment and one's own aspirations. It is only temporary whereas love is permanent.

Lust will create long-term issues in your life and your relationship, whereas love is a firm pillar that can allow a relationship to last forever. Lust is a temporary remedy for sexual desires, whereas love is permanent.

Most clients who are driven by lust demonstrate that their spouse is seen as an object rather than a person. Objects have no feelings and are therefore easy to abuse.

One of our clients shared his perspective on lust during a session. He advised that lust holds the key to fantasy. A man might imagine what a person looks like naked and what sex with them would be like.

The man doesn't think about what comes out of this person's mouth. The focus becomes her body and how he will seize the right moment to have her buy into his fantasy so that he can explore it. Some men might purchase flowers, do a fancy dinner or plan an elaborate romantic scheme, but only for the ultimate goal of having his sexual fantasies played out.

Some clients have said that if a woman refuses to engage in their fantasy, they seek to pursue more relationships to find someone who will. If he does have sex with the woman, he tries to find a way to stay disconnected.

The nature of lust is that when one has tasted of their fantasy and it has been fulfilled, they will crave more and want to explore something else. When it is fulfilled, lust pushes one's boundaries further and further. Unless a person is aware of this and is able to break the stronghold of lust, their mind will never stop thinking: *What if I did this way? What about that way? What about this person? What about that person?*

We have clients who have made a few attempts to engage emotionally with someone in the hopes that they will fulfill their fantasies and the moment they find that their fantasy is not going to be fulfilled they pull away. Clients who enter a relationship based on this desire to fulfill lust run when the person becomes too close or "cuddly." They refuse to engage in any form of commitment, especially if they are already married.

Lust cannot handle the sense of being close and committed. Love, on the other hand, would do everything to build an emotional bond. Lust makes one a predator and is constantly looking for its prey. Lust never stops unless a wind of reality blows by and the person is pulled out from their world of deceit.

Kathleen and I teach about what true love looks like. We tell couples that all solid relationships must be based on a genuine friendship that will eventually lead to love. True love can sustain a conversation that lasts for hours. I remember my first date with Kathleen where I did not want to leave Kathleen's presence. We met at around 5 p:00 p.m. and went out for dinner. We took a walk in Burlington Park near where she was living. We saw 2 swans side by side: one was black and the other was white. I thought of it as a sign that Kathleen would be my wife. As we spoke, everything about her captured my attention. The hours passed like minutes and before we knew it, we had been talking until 1:00 a.m.

When love is present, we see our spouse as a beautiful person in their entirety and not just on their exterior. We want to listen to them share about their day. We want to spend more time together. We picture a future together, buying groceries, raising a family and enjoying each other's company. We tell our friends, family and colleagues about them. This person is now the center of our life and all our plans are built and arranged to fit their schedule.

Love is a long-term journey that needs to be cultivated. As it unfolds, it is like a garden, which needs replenishing on a regular basis. It requires work. Lust on the other hand does not.

Love and lust can cross paths, especially when one first takes an interest in a person. However, as the relationship develops, the potential for it to last a lifetime is limitless if one matures past the stage of lust.

Socially, lust can ruin relationships even between good friends. Jealousy, pride and envy can stem from lust. Vocationally, lust can cause one to become competitive to the point of stepping on loved ones to attain one's goals. Lust can cause a person to lose their job if it leads them to a sexual relationship with the wrong coworker. Things could turn around and they can get charged for harassment. Psychologically, emotionally and socially lust leaves scars that cannot be erased and can harm present or future relationships directly or indirectly.

I encourage you to focus on building love and investing the time and effort that it takes to see love grow into something beautiful. Don't waste your seed on lust which has no value, is never fulfilled and can be disastrous socially, vocationally, psychologically and emotionally.

Points to Ponder:

1. What stimulates one to become sexually active?
2. How would you compare love to lust?
3. We learned how lust causes men to think with their bodies and not their hearts. How does this manifest itself in their relationships?
4. If love is "long-term", what is lust?
5. Can you imagine one scenario of lust gone wrong? In your opinion, would having engaged in that act of lust have been worth it?

MY STORY

I first came across the word "lust" back in Trinidad when I was 17 years old. I met someone who I felt was very special. We studied together every day for an entire semester. She was a beautiful girl, graceful and smart. I had never felt the way I felt with her with anyone else. I could not wait to meet her every day at 9:00 a.m. at the public library.

We were study buddies, but then I developed feelings for her. She was not of the same faith, but I convinced myself that she would one day convert and I resolved that I would try everything possible to make it happen. I thought of getting married at 18 years old since it would not have been shocking in my culture. (My grandmother was married at 12 and moved in with her husband at 14.)

A mature way of pursuing a relationship is establishing what it is that you want and waiting for it until it comes to you.

I was convinced that the girl and I would one day live happily ever after. If my parents did not agree with my decision, I would live with the girl in her parents' home (although I never met her parents). I thought that when we had children, my family would forgive me. I had it all figured out.

The girl had no problem wanting to get closer to me. Actually, there were no boundaries as far as she was concerned. I would have dreams about this girl and see images in my mind that were of a sexual nature. I was bothered by this so I went to my spiritual counsellor to share this with him, hoping that he would give me some insight.

As I poured my heart out to this well-respected mentor of mine, I was taken aback by his response. The first thing he asked me was, "How do you know you love her?" Then he asked, "Are you ready for a relationship?" I remember him saying that God created someone special for each person and that when we meet that person, nothing in the world could convince us less. The fact that I was feeling "possessed" with sexual desires by this girl's presence was a red flag for my mentor. He concluded that I was lusting after her and told me that this was not true love.

When my mentor told me that it wasn't true love, I became angry with him. I felt he was criticizing me and that he was making a wrongful judgment. After all, he did not know the girl. I didn't want to hear what he had to say and left his office at once.

I came to Canada for 6 months and the girl and I corresponded back and forth. Something was different though. I could feel from our conversations that something was not right, but ignored it.

I came back to Trinidad and we went out together. That day we had lots of laughs as we caught up. Even though we were having a great conversation, I could sense that something was wrong. Then in the midst of our conversation, she said with tears in her eyes, "I'm back with my old boyfriend." I could not believe what I was hearing. Here I thought we had a future together only to be told the relationship was over. I was crushed.

I could hear my last conversation with my mentor playing in my mind. I recalled a number of things he said: *love is long-term*; *love will stand by your side and never grow old*; *love has no end and always waits*. This was not love. It did not wait for me.

I could not believe that I was pondering having sex with this person and was considering breaking my faith and morals to do so. It was then that I realized that what we had was sexual desire and nothing more. I was captured by her beauty, her figure and the fact that she wanted to be with me.

When this girl betrayed me, I was utterly heartbroken, or I thought I was. I wanted to commit suicide. She had broken the rules.

She had not thought of my feelings. She allowed her past relationship to lure her, not thinking of the damage it would do to me. Her only words were, "I am sorry." After 6 months of investing my time in this person, this was very difficult to swallow. Who would I share my feelings with now? My heart felt like someone had taken it and stomped on it. I felt like my world had become empty and life had no purpose.

For a time, I could not see beyond what had happened. I could not envision a future without the girl. By the time I eventually migrated to Canada, I had told myself that I would remain single for the rest of my life. I had a firm belief that there was no one who could give me the emotional feelings that I considered to be love. However, I eventually began to feel the desire to have a close companion.

It felt difficult to engage in conversations with girls, as I felt that I would be heartbroken again. I tried going out on several occasions to connect with girls, but the risk of getting hurt again felt too great. My past was haunting me and hindering me from moving forward.

As a person who was brought up with strong family values, godly morals and good-old-fashioned traditions, I wrestled with the fact that I had considered giving in to my lusts.

After meeting Kathleen, I was reminded of the blessings that come with upholding the values, morals and traditions I cherish. God kept me just for Kathleen as I did not end up yielding to the flesh.

Although at the time I was disappointed with the choice the girl made, I would thank her today if I met her. I now know that she did me a favour when we separated.

I migrated to Canada and some years later I met Kathleen. When I met Kathleen, she was so different than all the other girls I had gone out with. When she would look me in the eyes, I felt that she could see into my soul. There was and still is something pure about her heart.

Kathleen radiated an angelic beauty. She is attractive, adroit, idealistic, virtuous, trustworthy, upright, temperate, righteous, truthful, undefiled, humble, puritanical, exemplary, abstemious, charming, amicable, kind, respectful, affable, servant-hearted, amiable, loving, suave, sweet, congenial, humorous, hospitable, courteous, polite, urbane and gracious. It is like God put my heart's desire into a reality in bringing her into my life.

About a month prior to meeting Kathleen, I went to a park close to my home and had a long conversation with God. I was living on my own, while my parents were in Trinidad. Apart from being lonely and missing my family, I was longing for a relationship. I had gone out with 4 girls over the period of 3 months but I knew that none of them were right for me.

When Kathleen came on the scene, it was like a prince meeting his princess. For weeks I thought it was a dream. As Kathleen proceeded to express her love for me without physical contact, I respected her even more. She broke the spirit of fear that held me bound for years. I had asked God for 12 specific qualities I wanted in the woman who would be my future wife and within the first 3 to 4 months, I saw them all in Kathleen. She was someone I would be proud to call my wife.

Kathleen was someone who could understand me. She expressed her love for me unconditionally. She loved me for who I was and treated me with respect. She was willing to be my friend. She stood with me in our shared faith and motivated me to press ahead spiritually. She brought comfort to me when I felt sad and lamented along with me. She rejoiced with me when I achieved accomplishments. She encouraged me to pursue my dreams. She had dreams of her own. She exhibited a passion for humanity, serving others and giving of herself. She endorsed sincerity and kindness on a level that I have never seen in anyone. It was evident that her heart had been polished by God, bearing the many fruits God is able to produce in a person. She treated me like someone of worth and I wanted to grow old with her.

The girl I thought I was in love with at 17 years old did not have these qualities, and to be honest, I never believed one person could actually carry all of these; I did make my request to God.

I knew that it would take only God to find a woman who would make me happy and keep me young at heart. A mature way of pursuing a relationship is establishing what it is that you want and waiting for it until it comes to you. I believe God has created a woman for every man. We need patience in waiting and searching for what we desire without crossing our own moral boundaries to attain it.

My relationship with Kathleen is such that I have often said that I wished that God would have given me 25 hours in the day so I could spend one more hour with Kathleen. When we wait for the right person who fits the desire in our heart, we begin our relationship on the right footing. The relationship will be built on love and not lust. It will possess the qualities that will sustain it for a lifetime.

Points to Ponder:

1. What is your story? What struggles did you have to overcome in order to conquer lust and invest in love?
2. What are you asking God for in your spouse?
3. How can knowing what you want in a spouse and waiting for it be a mature way of pursuing a relationship?

SETTING THE FOUNDATION

We usually enter into a relationship with the hope that it will last a long time. Things start off rather well. After the first year or so, all the flaws and weaknesses of our partner become evident. More time is spent at this early stage to maintain the relationship and address issues. Sooner or later, less time is invested and a couple might feel that they are fighting too much and their differences are not resolvable. They develop a belief that the relationship no longer suits their needs and they want to split up.

One man once said to me, a relationship is just a television. In a couple of years when you start having issues with it, you get rid of it and buy something better. However, it is possible that the old television could outlast the new one if fixed. This is what I believe relationships are like. As long as we

Like a building's foundation is made with certain materials such as concrete, stones, bricks, steel or mortar, the foundation of a relationship should be built with certain materials.

are willing to put some work in to fix them, they just might be worth our efforts.

A relationship is like an profitable investment. The longer you stay with it, the greater the interest. I am happy to say that with Kathleen and me, it appears that the older we become, the stronger our love for one another becomes. Like an investment, a relationship costs something. In this case, it costs us time, energy and a sincere effort in building a strong foundation.

In every relationship, there must be a solid foundation. To build our foundation, Kathleen and I have learned to assess what the most important aspects of the relationship are. We have identified our core values and what each other's needs are. Our foundation has helped us to avoid emotional affairs.

When I think of what a foundation is, I think of the commonalities a couple shares and the values they cherish. Some say that their foundation is based on love, trust, good communication, laughter, happiness or hope, and that is good. However, when I think of foundations, I get specific about these broad principles and think of family traditions, family values, faith, practices, personal likes and viewpoints that we share.

When couples start to accept constant bickering, arguing, emotional abuse, verbal abuse, backbiting and nasty comments there is definitely a problem. It will reach a point where it will happen in the open. This gives the impression to the younger generation and those watching that marriage is not valuable.

A proper foundation does more than just hold a relationship together. It keeps out anyone and anything that will bring hurt and pain into the relationship. It makes it far more likely that a relationship will last forever.

Like a building's foundation is made with certain materials such as concrete, stones, bricks, steel or mortar, the foundation of a relationship should be built with certain materials. Common values, joint goals and habits based on shared principles are some of the materials that must be used.

A good foundation requires more than digging a hole and pouring concrete into it. It must be tailored to the building that is being built upon it. Each relationship will have a unique make-up but the main materials will be the same.

No foundation can ever make a relationship 100% disaster-proof and the storms of life are bound to come. However, the stronger it is the more of a chance it can hold a couple through the tough times. The foundation might crack a little at some point, but it will not fall apart if it is laid properly.

Kathleen and I believe that relationship foundations should last forever so it makes sense to pay attention to the details when building. It ensures that the relationship holds together despite the storms that come.

Points to Ponder:

1. What can you do with a broken television instead of replacing it? How does this apply to a broken relationship?
2. How is a relationship like a profitable investment?
3. What makes up the foundation of a relationship?

EMOTIONAL AFFAIRS

When the foundation of a relationship is not solid or certain factors and boundaries are not in place, it opens the door for emotional affairs. An emotional affair is where a husband or a wife feels more comfortable sharing their personal issues with someone of the opposite sex other than their spouse. They develop a soul tie with this person and their spouse is no longer their best friend.

We are seeing more and more couples struggling with emotional affairs. The hurt from emotional affairs can be particularly painful and make it hard for a person to want to seek a resolution. However, when the basement in a house is flooded or the hot water tank is not working, the whole house is not considered to be a write-off. It is still fixable. Even a relationship that has suffered an emotional affair is worth salvaging.

There is a fine line between being kind and flirting and people in relationships must take care not to cross it regardless of how attractive a person might be.

Some couples have said to Kathleen and me that it is easier to get over a one-night stand than an emotional affair. I believe the main reason for this is because a one-night stand is meaningless and holds no value. It is done in a moment of lust. It involves no true feelings or personal thoughts. An emotional affair suggests a deeper connection and more meaningful feelings.

A man might seek an emotional affair when he finds common ground with another woman, especially when he is in a vulnerable state of mind. We all tread through rough waters sometimes. So it is important to distance oneself from others of the opposite sex, especially at these times.

A woman tends to seek out attention and admiration, which can lure her into an emotional affair. I told my daughter the other day, "You fell in love with that bird in the window of the store. How much more easy it is to fall in love with a man who expresses his affections for you." Like in *Beauty and the Beast*, a woman might potentially fall for any man who gives her the attention she needs. This is especially the case if she feels her spouse is not giving this to her.

A flirtatious mind can also lead to emotional affairs. There is a difference between being kind and concerned and being flirtatious. I have had to use charm on many occasions. I was bumped up to first class on an airplane by being extra friendly. The major difference is my wife was right by my side in this instance.

Some women give the impression that they are free for the taking and give men the wrong signal. Men have difficulty reading women in the first place and can get the wrong message. They push further and before they know it, an emotional affair has started. Of course, this work both ways and men have a tendency to flirt too.

There is a fine line between being kind and flirting and people in relationships must take care not to cross it regardless of how attractive a person might be. This includes using discretion when giving hugs and kisses.

When I speak to individuals or couples, I find there is never any intention to cheat or have an affair. Emotional affairs start small and build up gradually. Innocent phone calls, lunch with colleagues or "catching up" with someone from your past can be potentially disastrous to your relationship.

Trying to go back in the past with old friends or old neighbours you grew up with or making attempts to recreate old friendships with those of the opposite sex can be dangerous. When you are committed, every event revolving around the opposite sex should involve your spouse. Emotional bonds develop very easily. A person might have something in them you desire or feel your spouse is lacking.

It is important to be aware that something like this can lead to an emotional affair.

Emotional needs must be met in a relationship. When we consider a car, the engine might be well taken care off, but this doesn't mean the whole car is in good shape. There are other aspects of the car that also need attention. We need to clean the car regularly, change the tires and make sure there is gas in the tank. Although the engine is what determines the value of the vehicle, everything else needs to be in order as well. In a relationship, a couple might be having good sex and doing a good job of paying the bills together, but if the emotional part of the relationship is not in tact, the relationship is not whole and is vulnerable to an emotional affair.

One good strategy to avoid getting into emotional affairs is to draw an invisible line with others at your workplace. Avoid meeting colleagues on a regular basis, especially if you are dealing with personal issues. Venting your problems to another can lead to a relationship and this should be avoided. Meeting in groups will help to reduce the risk of having an emotional affair.

Another method of prevention is to have someone who can act as a coach or mentor in your lives as a couple. This person will help to examine the values at the core of your relationship and remind you of the value of the relationship itself. I believe every couple should find a coach or a mentor to help them to move ahead in their relationship. It will have tremendous value and give the couple motivation to stick together. This will eliminate the need to seek someone outside of the bounds of marriage for counsel or advice unnecessarily. Their accountability to their role model will provide a couple with the motivation necessary to succeed at suggestions or recommendations made.

Some preventative food for thought in order to avoid emotional affairs which can lead to sexual affairs or infidelity is establishing the freedom in the relationship to share your thoughts, feelings and opinions honestly with your spouse. Learning to listen to each other without being judgmental helps to balance privacy with intimacy appropriately in a relationship. Your life needs to be transparent like a projector slide to your spouse. When trust is developed it will become a solid rope that will tie your relationship together. With that being said, no individual should be forced to share their emails, letters or phone calls with their spouse. Respecting each other's privacy is important. However, there should not be anything that you cannot share with your spouse.

Make sure to express love physically, verbally and non-verbally to ensure that emotional needs are being met. This helps to ensure that the root causes behind emotional affairs are eliminated.

It is also good to know how to diffuse tense situations, rekindle passion and tug on the strings of your partner's heart. When Kathleen uses humour around me, it does something internal; it ignites my passions and the desire to love her grows even more.

Lastly, the notion of, "You do what you want and I do what I want," does not belong in a healthy relationship. Living separate lives only makes it easier for an emotional affair to creep in.

Points to Ponder:

1. Why is it important to have a coach or a mentor in your life as a couple? Who could play this role in your life?
2. How much about your personal issues should you share with your coworkers or colleagues?
3. How do emotional affairs begin?
4. What tugs on the strings of your partner's heart? Think of an incident in your relationship where using this to your advantage could have helped you get through a tight spot.

WHICH ROOM?

The heart is like a house with many rooms. In each room there is the capacity for more to belong than just one individual. Each room in our heart is for a different crowd of people. However there is one room reserved just for your spouse and your children.

I would like to start with the first room which I call the "acquainting" room. This room holds most of the people we feel comfortable with. It's a fairly large room since we allow people from different areas of life to come in. They might be people from work, school or church. They might be gym buddies, neighbours and friends.

> *The heart is like a house with many rooms.*

There is a place in this room for anyone you meet on life's journey and feel comfortable with.

Some of the people in this room might move to the next room in your heart which we will call the "like" room. The like room is much smaller than the acquainting room and only has the capacity to hold family members (immediate and extended) and close friends. It is those with whom you build a rapport that have a place in this room. Unfortunately, this room is one of the very few rooms you will have an excellent memory of and thus you are more vulnerable to those in it.

Some might house a place in this room for memories of people who hurt them emotionally. Perhaps they have had disagreements with people in this room and this has left a nasty smell or marks on the walls.

The like room requires the most maintenance since it needs cleaning on a daily basis. Hearts might be broken in this room and can cause lifelong scars.

The third room is the "love" room. This room I like the most since it has a nice aroma and has the brightest light. It affects all the other rooms. This is the room in which your spouse, your children and those friends who are like rare gems reside. Every couple needs to spend time exploring this room and keep up with its maintenance otherwise it can look dirty and dishevelled. It's from this room that deeper emotions are stirred. This room has a greater impact on feelings and can trigger great joy or dismay. This room is where romance lingers on.

The love room is the main room in every adult's heart. Some have locked the door to this room and pretend that it does not exist. Others enjoy this room but want someone else to clean up the mess.

This room has some of the best memories. It pushes the relationship to a higher degree of love. It's the room where couples store what they've learned about each other's likes and dislikes. This room is where communication flows from. It's like the library: a place where there's a lot to learn, lots to talk about and lots of future planning.

There are other rooms. The room that can affect a relationship the most is the room called "emotion" room. As its name suggests, this room is driven by emotions.

Most people operate from one room of the heart and might not see a need to learn about the entirety of the heart and what the other rooms hold. A healthy relationship is one in which each partner has discovered most of the rooms in their heart and considers the strengths of each one.

A healthy heart has the potential to foster healthy relationships. Each spouse in a relationship should be able to explore the rooms of the heart and work on cleaning the dust and dirt that has built up over time. When the rooms in the heart are identified and there is a determination to work on cleaning them up, the heart becomes healthy, creating healthy relationships.

We cannot change what has happened to us but we can clean our hearts. We need to search every room in our heart and decide which one might be in need of a cleanup or a renovation. The human heart will become alert and function effectively when we understand its anatomy.

Points to Ponder:

1. Which room harbours the most vulnerability and has the greatest potential to leave you with a broken heart?
2. Who resides in the "love" room of your heart?
3. Why should we explore and expose every room we find in our heart?
4. Can you think of a room in your heart that needs a general cleanup or a renovation?

LIFESAVERS

Kathleen and I have come to the conclusion that only God can be the main pillar in a healthy relationship. Resting on the pillars of God and love can bring about a long-lasting relationship that is filled with happiness and joy. We have an assurance that the God who created the universe without human help will help us through our weakness and helplessness.

Maybe you are in a current relationship where you are struggling. Regardless of where we are in life, God has a solution for every situation. He knows us all by name and He knows everything about us.

Don't stopping kissing the one you love.

Some have asked, "What else has kept your marriage fresh?" I like to answer that question by replying, "Have more children!" My other answer is that we do not point our fingers at each other concerning the problems that come up in our relationship. Some other suggestions we have recommended to couples that have sustained them through the ups and downs are the following.

1. Keeping Love Young

Having a joyful heart is good medicine. It keeps you healthy. For instance, it can keep you from getting heart problems or depression.

Having a joyful attitude is important in keeping your love alive in your relationship as well. The question we need to ask ourselves is, "How do we keep a joyful heart?"

We recommend that you "pucker up." Don't stopping kissing the one you love. Most of us remember being kissed by our parents, relatives and friends as babies. As we grow up, depending on the culture we greet each other with kisses. Some cultures greet with a kiss on one or both cheeks. Some kiss 3 times. In human culture as a whole, kissing has often been an expression of care and love.

In a relationship, kissing is very important. It stimulates the chemicals in the body that cause you to feel an attraction to someone. The downside to this is that some of us who are in a relationship and are not married might have struggles with premature passionate kissing. Kissing awakens all your emotions. You must be prepared to feel the sensation that will drive you to want to move to the next stage, from kissing to fondling and on to sex.

2. Having Fun Together

Having fun together and enjoying one another's company is a key to a successful relationship. When we were kids, we enjoyed playtime. In fact, playing is what we did with most of our free time as children.

Fun keeps the soul alive. Small gestures, remarks and fun activities can make a world of difference in a relationship. Fun lightens the burdens faced along the journey of life.

One example (a true story), that I always remember is taken from the late 1800's. It's a story about a man by the name of Smith Wigglesworth who became one of the greatest healing evangelists of his time. At the start of his marriage, his wife was the evangelist and would travel to different cities and churches preaching and teaching. Smith would remain at home taking care of the children. He backslid a bit from the church and the small things in his relationship began to irritate and consume him.

One evening his wife arrived home quite late as she was accustomed to, but this was one more thing to irritate Wigglesworth. As she came through the front door, Smith grabbed her and pushed her back out, locking the front door. This did not deter Polly, his wife, and she marched around the house and entered through the back door laughing as she came in.

This broke the ice around Wigglesworth's heart and he joined her in laughing. This moment of relief brought Wigglesworth back to ministry alongside his wife. Her reaction to a potentially disastrous situation changed the direction of their relationship and ministry.

Couples need to learn how to have fun together. Playing cards together, having lunch, making out in a parking lot (Kathleen and I have been caught on several occasions), kissing in elevators, visiting the office spontaneously or simply walking in a park once in a while can add fun and can rekindle the sparks of joy in a relationship.

Teasing, touching and using our awkward moments as opportunities to create laughter will lighten the mood in the relationship and build upon the relationship's foundation. Sometimes we might become upset or overwhelmed with the silliest things and when we can laugh about them, we ask ourselves, *Was that worth all the fuss?* Laughter is the best ice-breaker, heart-mender, tear-wiper and stress-reliever. It has every right to play a vital role in a relationship.

3. Staying Attractive

So what does exactly does "staying attractive" mean? Well, we have all seen or experienced the process when a person begins a relationship and they spend a great deal of time on trying to look good, from buying new clothes to working out in the gym and going through great lengths to achieve a clean look. However, as a relationship ages, individuals often have the tendency to stop looking after themselves.

People often complain that their spouse's hygiene and grooming habits "have gone down the drain." Their spouses no longer shave their faces, legs or underarms. They ignore grey hairs, say they want to look "natural" or wear outdated clothes. They might not take care to wash clean, they might gain weight, fail to coordinate their outfits or just throw on whatever clothes they can find. An excuse that we often hear from couples is, "We cannot help it. We are too busy with work and the kids."

Self-esteem tends to deteriorate and health problems can even develop when we don't take care of ourselves. We need to realize that in a relationship maintaining our bodies and a decent outward appearance is part of our duty to one another.

We should never stop trying to look our best for our spouse or partner. If we want them to keep their eyes on the one they love, we need to look the best we can. The object is to always aim to look your best and better than the next couple you meet.

Wearing blue jeans and a t-shirt might not always cut it when you are going out for a nice, romantic candlelight dinner. We need to maintain a level of respect for one another where we put effort into looking good for one another. Failing to do this is like wearing red to a funeral or a three-piece suit to the beach. This is the key to staying attractive. Whether we have grey hair, get a receding hairline or add a few extra pounds we are still beautiful to our spouse when we try.

4. Engaging In Physical Contact

The human body craves touch and intimacy. As children, we grew up giving and receiving touch, reacting and responding to the stimulation it brings. When children are left alone and are not touched they withdraw and close themselves off to the world around them. We see this happening in orphanages where children are left alone for hours on end. It requires a long and arduous process to enable these children to develop healthy relationships and intimacy as they grow up.

Simple acts of touch can communicate so much. An action like holding hands together brings a sense of belonging, security and protection. Nothing is wrong with walking into the kitchen and putting your arms around your spouse. He or she is of your own flesh.

5. Being Able To Adapt and Compromise

There are a lot of things that we need to learn to adapt to in relationships. We also need to learn the concept of compromise.

We have had people tell us that their spouse watches too much T.V. and does not want to go out. They complain that their partner is a couch potato and does not socialize with others. The other partner might find that their spouse likes to go out or socialize too much. We have encouraged spouses in such relationships to spend some time with their spouses watching more television than they might like and then in turn, we encourage their spouses to go out shopping or for ice cream once in a while.

Men especially, if your spouse wants to go shopping, take that opportunity to spend time together and go with her even if it's not what you like to do. A relationship cannot be one person's way all the time and still be healthy.

6. Building a Godly Legacy

This one is for those with children or who are planning to have them one day. Truly what we invest into our children, the example we set and the principles we hold dear are the riches we have as a family; an inheritance like no other. We should desire to leave a legacy behind us. We should want our children to have the same strong relationship we have as a couple if not stronger.

Kathleen's parents sowed prayers into our lives and we have inherited that legacy and can now pass it down to our children. We want to see that our children will continue in the ways of the Lord and pass it down to their own children.

If you have grown children already and you are praying for your family, don't get discouraged. Your prayers are sowing into their relationships and you are sowing into future relationships down the line at the same time.

We cannot determine our children's choices in the future but we can determine our choices as a couple. We can set the foundation for our children. They will eventually have to make the choice whether to build upon it or not. Either way we have done our part in giving them a good example to follow. Working to build a godly legacy together as a couple blesses the relationship and strengthens the entire family.

7. Living Each Day As If It Were the Last

Enjoy each moment as a couple. Take pleasure in the time spent together and try to make it special for one another. Find things to do together that are going to create memories; the memories you will hold on to fondly and treasure.

There will always be obstacles along your path and situations that can deter you or your spouse in your journey as a couple. It helps to have memories together than you can refer to in times of trouble and to be in the habit of creating such memories for when they are needed.

Some couples we have counselled were on the verge of handing over their wedding rings. We have had clients who made plans to go to shelters and even to leave the country to escape from their relationship issues. However, we have seen examples of couples like these that have turned their relationships around completely by being open to trying our relationship lifesavers.

Points to Ponder:

1. Name some suggestions to keep a relationship fresh and the love strong. Can you think of some specific ways you can apply these suggestions to your relationship with your spouse?
2. How does learning to laugh at our mistakes and stressful situations help us in our relationships?
3. What type of inheritance do you want to leave for your children through your relationship?

COMMITMENT COMPELLS

To some people, commitment means wearing a ring and being "tied down" to one person for the rest of their lives. The "what ifs" govern their mind and to play it safe, they decide to stay unmarried and just live together.

Commitment has means much more than just being legally bound together. A couple just living together can separate more easily than a married couple. A married couple has a better chance of working out relationship issues due to the commitment made to each other publicly and under God. The ring on our finger reminds us of the choice we made to be with the person we chose to love.

Being in a committed relationship can have the effect of helping one to achieve their goals so goals should never be seen as a prerequisite for commitment.

Commitment is a very powerful piece of armour with a definite purpose. It is the shield that protects one's emotional state of mind. It prevents mental health issues from developing later down the line as well as psychosomatic stressors.

Commitment is a foundational pillar Kathleen and I focus on in relationship counselling. We focus on it in each relationship we support. Without it there is no hope of a lasting relationship.

Commitment looks at all avenues that will build a better level of relationship. It looks at all the reasons as to why it is important to compromise or meet each other half way when there are differences of opinion. A consensus is made to resolve issues rather than suppress them. Commitment looks at growth and purpose instead of running away or ignoring reality.

A number of people are of the opinion that marriage is old-fashioned and only prevents one from experiencing the world to the fullest. On the contrary, there are many benefits to being in a relationship with the same person. We need to remember that the person we age with becomes wiser and can be much more fun to be with as time goes by. They know you better than anyone else and, hopefully, you know them just as well. When I think of Kathleen and myself, I can attest to the fact that our relationship has soared to new levels as time has passed. Our relationship has only become better over the years.

Living in the past instead of the future seems to be a common observation among people who avoid commitment. Some people have difficulty letting go of others in their past. Some people, and particularly men, have an expectation or desire for their spouse to be like their parents, ex-spouse or best friends and like to make comparisons.

There are other common reasons why people don't commit. Individuals in a relationship can have unattainable goals, like wanting to be a millionaire by get-rich-quick schemes or to become an idealized version of themselves before they commit to a relationship.

Being in a committed relationship can have the effect of helping one to achieve their goals so goals should never be seen as a prerequisite for commitment. When Kathleen and I were newly married, I only had a high school diploma and was not career-oriented. I worked various unrelated jobs. I was as a drywall taper, a mushroom farm worker and also a tobacco farm worker. I sold vacuums, life insurance and worked as a photo technician.

I completed 2 years at a Bible College, did mission trips, pastored, planted churches, travelled to different countries and did a tour from Ontario to Alberta speaking at different churches. Though we were helping to motivate and guide others, I ignored the fact that we were living on pennies and the bills were growing larger as our family was growing.

It took about 7 years after being married, but I eventually came to the realization that I needed to set an example to our children and focus. I enrolled in school full-time, studied through the summer, fall and winter semesters and worked as much as I could. Ministry became secondary and the family became my primary focus. Driving a school bus, studying and working nights at a halfway house, I kept my focus on creating a stable family. I was committed to my wife and children and there was no easy way out.

I eventually completed 2 master's degrees and a PhD and graduated with honours, obtaining recognition by the Summa Cum Laude. I am not saying that each individual needs to do exactly what I did. Educational success was an area I needed to conquer in my life. (For me, it was a matter of breaking the familial curse of underachieving educationally as my parents and grandparents did not complete school.

Being in a committed relationship under the covenant of marriage can look restrictive, but I believe it is the more beneficial option. Couples that take the step of getting married are more likely to stay together. The enjoyment experienced between 2 committed people can expand over time and the bond created can motivate an individual to conquer their personal mountains in life, whatever they might be.

Points to Ponder:

1. When a couple makes a commitment in public, does it put them in a better position to work out issues when they arise?
2. Learning to identify some of the causes behind failure to commit is important. What are some of these?
3. Why should commitment be considered a powerful piece of armour?

A RELATIONSHIP
HEADED DOWNHILL

Every relationship that is healthy started on a good note. If yours was started on anything other than a good note, you might be in the relationship for the wrong reasons. Some have expressed that after being together for over 15 years they didn't think anyone would love them, so they went for the first person who showed some interest in them. This puts extra stress on a relationship. However, such a relationship is still salvageable with the appropriate relationship counselling.

A relationship that is clearly heading downhill is one that is abusive. We must remember: once a zebra, always a zebra. We can paint a zebra to look like a cow, but its nature doesn't change. The zebra might adapt, just as culture, the environment or ethnic background can enable us to adapt and behave differently than our natures

A relationship that is clearly heading downhill is one that is abusive.

prescribe. However, it is more likely that the zebra will take on its inherent nature. It is possible for a zebra to act like a cow with the right conditioning and you might be waiting on an abusive spouse to get help and change. However, unless that time comes, your waiting can last a lifetime.

Kathleen and I have been successful in helping individuals come out of abusive relationships and seek appropriate support. It is important to avoid abusive relationships as it is easier to run downhill than to climb uphill.

We see various couple's that seem like they are going downhill. Partners wait until they hit rock bottom and then look for support. Sometimes, support is sought so late that the partners have given up hope on moving ahead or have spent their energy to the point of exhaustion.

There are some common scenarios that bring a couple to the point where they feel they are headed downhill fast. Sometimes a person might be threatened by their spouse or partner's success and pride and jealously might build up towards their spouse. This should not be the case. Both partners in a relationship have a vision and the visions should complement one another's rather than pull down the relationship. A spouse should never make their partner feel guilty for succeeding in life, especially since the success is to be shared.

Some couples start the process of descent when a major change takes place. I use the prime example, "He is no longer working, so who will take care of me?" or, "She is too sick to care for my needs anymore."

Couples struggling in a relationship might have lost the "loving feeling"—that feeling that gives the butterfly sensation in one's stomach and where one cannot wait to be with their spouse when separated. I remember meeting with Kathleen for the first time. There was a cocktail of sex hormones running up and down my emotional walls. The testosterone and estrogen levels were increasing by the second. She was "hot!"

The more we conversed with each other, the more we were stimulated, increasing the desire to be with one another. We spent hours upon hours on the phone. When we had coffee or dinner, we did not want the night to end. The increased level of dopamine and serotonin removed any feelings of depression or anxiety. My adrenaline levels increased and I had the feeling that I could conquer the world. Kathleen made me feel that I could walk through any fire or climb any mountain. Her very presence caused my heart to beat faster. I was lost in the arms of love.

The issue starts with trying to maintain the increased level of dopamine and serotonin throughout the relationship without a knowledge and application of the effort that it takes. Most couples when they have passed the stage of initial satisfaction with each other and sex with each other is no longer new begin to see the imperfections in their partner. Once hormone levels are back to normal, couples feel like they are living with a friend or an enemy rather than their soul-mate or their lover.

Poor communication is a relationship downer that tops the list. People in relationships often share that they want to be heard. A partner needs to be validated and reassured that their spouse understands them.

Some couples have shared that sex is the number one issue in their marriage. Most men would agree they are not having enough sex. Men, particularly, might end up turning to someone else or something else for sex. We did a survey of 100 married men aged 19 to 45 and found that 87% felt that sex had been an issue in their marriage at one time or another. The other 13% either stated that they had experienced sexual dysfunction or refused to answer.

Some men have stated that they turn to the internet, pornography, sex shops and one-night stands. Others simply ignore the issue. Sex is not discussed enough in most relationships and when the issue becomes a problem, most women feel obligated to have sex just to please the man. Nothing is wrong in having a sex therapist to give some advice.

Lack of time spent together in a relationship can eventually cause a couple to feel like it has reached the point of no return. Quality time is important in maintaining a healthy relationship. With the pressure in today's society to work longer hours and easily accessible emails, phone calls and text messages, time is easily taken away. I made a rule to myself a few years ago that whenever I am at home, I will take only calls from family or close friends. I do not bring my work home, nor will I use my home time for someone else that might not have much value when compared to the relationship. My wife and children are number one when I am at home and everything else can wait. After all, I am not 911.

Financial issues can often lead to separation. I had some financial issues in my relationship which I can only believe stemmed from the way I grew up. My parents were poor. We lived in a village with no running water or electricity, so every penny had great value. I learned to appreciate money. Kathleen on the other hand, was working from an early age and was independent. Money was not a big issue for her. Couples need to realize it is "not my money" but ours and compromise on how the subject of money is approached in the relationship.

Whether it's a change in the dynamics of the relationship, the loss of that butterfly feeling, sickness, sex or financial issues, there are no reasons to walk away from a relationship where months and years were invested, unless the commitment was not consummated or the relationship is abusive.

Relationships go through seasons and sometimes like the winter season, everything feels dry and dead, however, there is still life in the dry plants and there are fertile bulbs sitting in the ground even in the harshest of winters. All relationships should be focused on moving ahead into sunnier seasons and moving up to higher heights.

Relationships are analogous to a mountain, where healthy ones head upwards. The longer we take to start heading towards the mountain top, the more painful the climb up to the top.

Points to Ponder:

1. Can you describe a relationship that looks like it's going downhill?
2. Why is it important to maintain and/or increase the level of dopamine and serotonin in your relationship?

RECREATION AND COMPANIONSHIP

Most couples prior to getting married plan activities that involve some form of recreation. Kathleen and I officially met while roller-skating. We played volleyball and baseball together, watched hockey and soccer games as we dated. Many couples make efforts to enjoy each other's recreational lifestyles before marriage but once married, this stops.

Recreation and companionship are important emotional needs, which open the love bank so relationships can flow into romantic love. Recreation in general is a healthy thing to do. It causes chemicals to flow in the brain that reduce stress or the roots of depression.

Many couples make efforts to enjoy each other's recreational lifestyles before marriage but once married, this stops.

Recreation should not possess our lives, but there should be a balance. It's not the same to sit and watch a sport show on television as it is to be with someone watching a game in a change of environment with hundreds of stimulants for the brain to absorb. Seeing the emotions of people as they smile, laugh, cry and shout creates a memorable experience. The different colours of clothes, sparkly items, paints on the walls, new smells, etc., are all stimulants. Balloons blown up, people in groups and people of different backgrounds all bring different stimulants to the brain. It awakes the brain and brings a flow of energy through the body. The emotions grow, especially the emotions of love.

We have couples that have difficulty understanding the need to have recreation in their relationships. One spouse might want to get involved in some type of sport and the other adamantly refuses. Instead of supporting each other, an emotional wound takes place and it becomes infected. A little issue becomes a big problem.

I worked with a couple who was in their late 40's where the female developed some friends from working out at the gym. She allowed her time to be stolen from her spouse, as most of the others in the group were single. (This female was married for 21 years with 3 children.) She had been unemployed and spent most of her time at home.

By being encouraged to join the gym, a membership was purchased. This female chose to go to the gym after 5:00 p.m. when her other friends would join her after their jobs. One child had baseball, the other had soccer and the oldest had a study group. The husband worked 8:00 a.m. to 4:00 p.m. For the past 21 years, the husband would arrive home and be greeted by his wife and 3 beautiful children. All of this changed after the gym membership was purchased.

The husband would come to an empty home. No food was prepared. The house would appear disheveled and untidy. The laundry would pile up for weeks. There were dishes in the sink from the previous day. The bed was always unmade. The washroom was dirty. Sometimes the dog would not be fed and would urinate on the floor. At times, feces would be visible as a result of no one taking the dog out for a walk.

Each person enjoyed their lifestyle except the husband. Several conversations were made, however, no one took up the slack. The wife had joined a sports team with her friends that demanded her time. Their daughter who was 18 years old found out that she was pregnant. The oldest son failed his final exams in university and the 16-year-old got into a relationship with a 32 year old married male.

The family started to fall apart. The husband felt powerless and started to pick up extra shifts at work. No one saw that there was a problem except the husband. The wife kept saying to her husband, "You worry too much. We will have a family day next week." Next week never came for over 8 months. The pregnant daughter had an abortion and her boyfriend left the scene. The oldest child threatened to kill himself and the 16 year old ran away from home. There were several females who made passes at the husband. However, he ignored them all. He used alcohol as his way of coping and would drink himself to sleep.

What do you think went wrong with this family and what should have been done? Evidently, this problem grew to the point where the family fell apart and there was little to no communication. Whenever the couple was home together, they avoided each other or spent time on the computer, cell phones or electronic devices. They were putting the blame on each other for not spending time together. There was no form of conversation or discipline with the children.

One day when the whole family was home, the husband called a meeting to discuss the issues. As he started to address what he saw was taking place in the home, the other family members totally ignored him. The client's wife started to yell and scream and blamed him for not being at home and not addressing the issues with the children.

The 18-year-old started to cry, stating that she felt alone and like garbage. She did not feel like living as she had killed a life. She had fallen into depression and had been sleeping most of the day trying to avoid thoughts of what she did by having the abortion. The oldest son shared about not having any mentorship or leadership in his life. He felt like his parents did not care about him and he shared how he had made plans to hang himself later on that day. He had even purchased rope from a hardware store and made a noose, which he had hidden in his bedroom.

The youngest daughter opened up about the struggles she had been going through, expressing that she was raped on several occasions when alone with the man she was seeing. On one occasion, she went to visit him and he had 3 of his friends over to play cards. They were all in their late 30's and early 40's and took turns having sex with her. The man that she thought loved her watched as his friends had their way with her. He told the 16-year-old he loved her and would give her whatever she wanted, adding that he enjoyed seeing others have sex with her. She told her parents that she went to the pharmacy and was planning to overdose on medications and jump over a bridge located a few kilometers from the city.

The father stood in shock as he heard what was going on in the lives of his family members. His wife responded by telling the children they needed to grow up and stop looking for attention. She then said it was getting late and her friends were waiting for her. Before leaving, she began to divulge by saying that she had been enjoying her friends because they showed interest in her life and supported her at the gym. She shared her frustration that no one understood that she needed to exercise. As you can see, the wife was frustrated that no one in her family seemed to care about her life and what she wanted. Her gym friends offered companionship over volleyball and curling, things she liked to do.

The husband responded by saying, "I became a workaholic as a result of you," addressing his wife as he shared his frustration. She stopped and vented and expressed that it was the husband's fault that he deliberately avoided her, did not support her or ask about her life. She said that her husband was too much into his own world, watching television, playing video games, texting, working and not sharing time with the family. She argued that the husband was self-absorbed and avoided the subject of supporting others in the family.

The husband expressed that he could not "make love to a block of ice," and someone who made everyone "feel like crap." He had been doing everything to maintain the home while his wife spent most of her time at the gym or with her friends.

The argument escalated to the point where the husband decided to pack his bags and leave, requesting for his 3 children to leave with him. They all packed their bags and left with their father to a hotel. The wife threw a tantrum and went up to her room screaming, "Nobody cares about me! Nobody cares about me!"

With everyone in the car ready to go, the husband went back to the house to grab his eyeglasses and overheard his wife saying to someone on the phone, "My husband left me with the children and I don't know what to do," adding, "I love him and don't know what I did for us to become like strangers."

The husband waited till the conversation was over and asked his wife if she understood why he was leaving. She responded by saying that she was aware that things had not been the same lately but she was willing to change. She went on to say that he had not been there for her and she found friends who enjoyed activities with her. The husband told his wife that he was looking for the same. As it turns out, the husband spent the night at a hotel but returned the next day. Both of them had some time to think about their lives and what they wanted.

The couple met with us, discussed their future together and spoke about compromising and supporting each other's needs. The husband explained to his spouse the need for recreation to be experienced within the family unit and not just individually. He explained that he had initiated the gym membership for family time and time together as a couple, not for others.

When you think of recreation, think of any activity you or your spouse love and would like to be engaged in. Recreation helps us feel refreshed. It gives the mind a break and spices up the daily routine.

Some outdoor activities to consider are hiking, scuba diving, swimming, golf, walking, boating, beach games, ball games, fishing, museum visits, amusement parks, photography, sight-seeing, gardening, concerts and the list goes on.

Some indoor activities are dancing (Kathleen and I did it when she was 7 months pregnant), musical concerts, movies, indoor gardening, watching T.V., playing board games, aerobics, bowling and billiards games. These are just a few of many.

Recreational activities will bring you, your spouse and your children closer together. More time invested in the relationship doing activities under the umbrella of recreation will strengthen the bonds of companionship within the family and maximize your potential to kiss breakups goodbye.

Points to Ponder:

1. How is recreation and companionship an emotional need?
2. What are 2 things that happen when a couple engages in recreation together?
3. What type of recreation do you enjoy? Is it a shared activity with your spouse?

KISSING BREAKUPS GOODBYE

There is no such thing as a perfect relationship or a perfect marriage. When 2 people first come together, their hearts are still their own, however, when they decide to live together, their hearts no longer belong to them, but their spouses. Two people living together are bound to get annoyed, irritated or frustrated with each other some time or the other. Within 3 months of living together, you begin the journey of becoming more aware of each other's flaws, weaknesses and differences in upbringing and opinions.

From leaving the toilet seat up to leaving dishes in the sink, there a number of potential irritants that will make you wonder why you got married and why you did it with the one you're with. However, it's important to keep focus and stick with the choice you made. Take on the attitude that it's only going to get better. There is no need to panic, or to call your friends or family. All of this is normal and most couples go through this process.

> *From leaving the toilet seat up to leaving dishes in the sink, there a number of potential irritants that will make you wonder why you got married and why you did it with the one you're with.*

The process of adjusting to a new life with your partner is like having your first child. At first, everything you do revolves around your child, from the purchases you make to decorating the baby room to baby-proofing the house. When your baby is born, you become very cautious with regards to who holds him or her. You attend to the baby every time he or she cries or has a wet diaper. You monitor their sleep patterns and eating habits and visits to the doctor are made regularly. You make sure everything is done by the book. After becoming familiar with the routine, you don't make so much of a fuss.

Marriage is the same. We start out by doting over our partners and then somewhere along the way things lose their excitement. The problem most couples have is they run away from the issues with their spouses or get the wrong advice from those who are not professionals or who are biased.

All of the suggestions presented in this book can help you to kiss breakups goodbye for good. In this chapter, I want to emphasize that it is not your specific relationship that is uniquely affected by the majority of problems you face. There are some issues that are common to all relationships when we share a life together with the one we love.

One issue we see in relationships we call the "drifter disorder." I was sitting by the lake one summer when I identified this disorder. I saw a piece of wood floating on the water As the wind blew, it came closer to the shore. The waves were determining the destination of that piece of wood.

As I pondered on this, I began to see the piece of wood as a hideout for fish, plants and birds. The wood was assisting many others.

We see in some relationships the husbands or the wives are like a piece of wood floating on a lake. The "wind" and "waves" of life can carry us away to the point where we psychologically and emotionally drift away from our partner (the shore). These same individuals who are the drifters, might be assisting others around them and will offer support as much as needed to other people in their life, but will neglect their own. The pressure in the relationship creates waves which cause them to drift away from the one they love.

The "faucet syndrome" happens when our partner seems to become more like a leaky faucet to us than a working tap. A well-functioning faucet is a luxury that provides the necessity of water as well as makes life much easier. Like a leaky faucet, with the "faucet syndrome," your spouse can become annoying to you to the point where you can loose sight of their importance and the benefit of having them around. The partner leaks drip by drip like the leaky faucet that never gets fixed and often becomes the loudest sound in the room.

Another issue we identify as the cause of breakups in a relationship is the "dehumidifier effect." We have a dehumidifier in our basement, which broke at one time. I have come to learn that a dehumidifier reduces the level of humidity in the air and eliminates dank smells. Before coming to the knowledge of the role of the dehumidifier, we had noticed that one corner of our basement wall had mold and mildew. We went to the home hardware store and were told the cause was that the home was too humid.

Not only was there unsightly mold and mildew, but the extra humidity made the children uncomfortable. They had difficulty sleeping and the pipes in the basement were dripping from condensation.

I like to associate a dehumidifier with some people in relationships. Sometimes it feels like the relationship is humid, creating mold and mildew. Couples live uncomfortably with each other and lose sleep over the issues that are infecting the relationship.

The dehumidifier can be one of the parties in the relationship who tries to put things in order. This person might feel overworked as they try to keep the relationship alive. They are the one seeking counsel, compromising, making attempts to communicate, creating structure in the home, seeking spiritual support and looking for all the possible solutions to the issues in the relationship.

This can become tedious and sooner or later, they break down. If you notice that you are the dehumidifier in the relationship, there needs to be a conversation regarding the sharing of responsibility in the relationship.

Another class of issues we call the "seasonal disorder." Working in mental health, we usually see individuals suffering seasonal disorders, or SAD, during the fall and winter. This can even stretch out to late spring or early summer. I was told by several psychiatrists that hormonal changes, reduced sunlight and foods high in carbohydrates can cause seasonal disorders.

I see seasonal disorders more frequently in women than men, where a woman might become irritable and "out of sorts." Some have presented with debilitating symptoms which interfere with their everyday life and their relationships.

While on the subject, I'd like to remind that some couples have difficulty adjusting to the different "seasons" of their relationship. Seasons such as career changes, the loss of a job, poor health, children leaving the home, poor finances and aging bring about circumstances that we must grow and adapt to. These can be stressful and if you don't force yourself to adapt they can greatly impact your health and relationships.

The "tornado effect" is another disorder we have identified in relationships. One summer Kathleen and I and the children were down at Myrtle Beach and for the first time, we saw a real-life tornado formatting at sea. There were actually a few distinct tornados forming different shapes and sizes. We could feel the wind getting stronger and everyone had to look for cover.

It was strange since it was a bright summer day when within minutes the atmosphere changed and the sun disappeared. Families were running frantically as the storm got stronger. The appearance of the storm was scary. The thunder, intensity and its unpredictability had people in panic mode.

The relationship can look wonderful at times. All appears to be going well. Then suddenly, with a slight change of mood or difficult circumstance, the relationship quickly becomes problematic. The light in the relationship disappears suddenly as we hear the sound of thunder and the storm approaches.

Kathleen and I had our share of difficult circumstances in the early stage of our marriage. We travelled a lot, stayed in the homes of people we did not know, slept in a foreign country at a train station in the winter, were physically and emotionally attacked, were removed from our home with the children in the middle of the night on account of our faith, endured death threats, were stoned, financially drained, and the list can go on and on. But, we kept moving ahead working out the issues as they came our way because we knew that troubles could come along even if things looked okay on the surface.

Lastly, it is important to discuss the "rollercoaster effect," which touches on some of the other effects. This is another source of issues I see in relationships. When we think of a roller coaster we think of people screaming in a ride and going up and down on a track. Roller coasters rely on basic inertial and gravitational forces to create an experience. The experience can be thrilling and fascinating, and it can also cause people to become sick.

Kathleen and I see some couples approaching relationships the wrong way which has the rollercoaster effect. You know by now that there will always be ups and downs in a relationship. Two people merging together to become one is not an easy task. There must be lots of compromising and adjusting on every level of the relationship.

A roller coaster can have 2 effects. It can be enjoyable when one knows what the ride is all about and is prepared for the ups and downs. For a person who knows what to expect, there is a sense of thrill and fascination. The other effect is an individual can become sick and tired of the ride and want off because of a lack of foresight or expectation that the ride will be wild.

I believe educating oneself about the nature of relationships so that there is not the expectation that it's going to be a "happily ever after" fairy tale can result in something special.

Points to Ponder:

1. How does educating yourself before entering relationships prepare you for the real thing?
2. How does knowing that other couples are experiencing many of the same issues as you make you feel?

CO-DEPENDENCY
AND PASSIVITY

Men are conditioned from birth to seek the approval of women. Most men are raised by women, and are told what to do and what not to do by their mothers. When they begin school, most of their teachers from kindergarten right up to college or university are females.

Many men grow up in homes without fathers. Some that do have fathers might never see them as the fathers, since most are busy spending their time working to make ends meet. The male grows up and develops his idea of manhood from male friends who have the same struggles. He becomes rebellious or stubborn to fit this false notion of manhood or to avoid being looked down upon.

The relationship should never be more important to a person than one is to oneself.

A man's nature can easily be mishandled by some females who believe they can give the best advice and impart life's principles. Women will do the best they can as mothers, friends, sisters or other family members. They might also do just fine as professional advisors and counsellors to implement positive notions of manhood. However, this often has the effect of developing a form of psychological training that teaches that saying and doing what women want rather than what is needed to survive as a man is adequate.

Those who are empowered by females will develop good life principles about how to treat women and care for those they love. However, their psychological defence mechanisms can become weakened and they might be more passive in nature as a result. Passivity is best described as the possession of a perilously limited will. A man whose psychological defence mechanisms are weakened will either try to avoid conflicts, defend himself unduly or get taken advantage of by others more often. They will see no need to share what they really want, need or think either.

We have met couples where the man depends on his spouse for a good portion of his happiness and success, yet finds it difficult to express his real feelings as to the need to draw closer to her. He feels that expressing himself might unravel the inner person, exposing his weaknesses and creating the opportunity for him to be rejected.

Negative feelings or observations can get stuffed down for long periods of time. When a passive man eventually builds up the courage to express his true feelings to his spouse or ex-spouse it might be too late. It can look like an awakened volcano has erupted. It takes a lot of pressure to erupt, however, once erupted, it's like an explosion that might surprise his spouse and those close to him. He reaches the point where he feels he no longer has anything to lose and therefore lets loose, but it might seem to the spouse like it is coming from left field.

When a woman sees her spouse who is usually quiet with few words become assertive and vocal, this can be shocking and difficult to accept. She might make the assumption that he is cheating on her or having an affair. She might also think that he has developed a lack of interest in her or is getting old.

When couples come for counselling, the importance of identifying who "wears the pants in the home" becomes evident. When a home has 2 heads, there will be issues as there will always be "2 heads butting one another." It makes it difficult to compromise and the relationship will fall apart. I like to suggest to couples that even though the man in the house might be laid back and passive, he should still at least be leading the family along with his spouse. If not, it rejects his true nature and his actual identity, and hides what's left of himself from others.

I often see male clients who think of themselves as disposable. Most of these men who are raised by women, not only carry the message that their fathers are expendable, but that they are detrimental to the family.

T.V. sitcoms add to this. They portray men as incompetent husbands and fathers, buffoons either to be set straight or cast aside. The media has perfected the concept that men have spiralled into bewildered and lowly creatures. The impression given today in our society and culture is that men are useless and only good for sperm. Their love, their time and their guidance are superfluous. They are now called "sperm donors." What would happen if women were called "breeders?"

I believe that fathers play a major role in fostering the well-being of their children, not only by being providers, but protectors and figures who establish guidance. Men need to feel that it is okay to express how they feel without being put down. It will build their self-esteem and confidence. The relationship should never be more important to a person than one is to oneself. Expressing oneself assertively and according to one's nature is a benefit for the individual, the relationship and the family as a whole.

In relationships where a man might be passive and laid back, his spouse should be complementing him and allowing the world to see that he's the best thing that happened to her. A woman might be passive. The same applies to her, where her husband should show to the world that she is the best thing that happened to him.

Anyone living in relationship with a passive person will find themselves in a co-dependent relationship. Such a relationship can become comfortable and a person might feel they are unable to live alone. You might think co-dependency serves the relationship, but co-dependency will cripple your relationship as your spouse becomes self-absorbed and uninterested in your needs.

Points to Ponder:

1. When men are raised by females alone how can it lead to passivity?
2. What can happen to a passive man who bottles up his feelings?
3. How does culture and today's society today affect the role of men in relationships?

LOVE AFFAIRS AND SEXUAL SHAME

So many individuals struggle with wanting more in their relationships that it is becoming an epidemic. Kathleen and I are seeing more and more individuals and couples struggling with sexual promiscuity. Some have expressed that they are being sexually satisfied with their spouses. It's just that they find sex as a way of coping when under stress.

The most frequent question Kathleen and I have been asked in our seminars is, "Why is there cheating in a relationship?" or "How do you know when your spouse is having an affair? We have seen multiple couples where this has been a very big issue in their relationship.

As a general rule, if I cannot do something in front of my spouse, then it's not worth doing it behind her back.

When your spouse becomes unfaithful it poses a great problem in the relationship. It breaks the cover of trust. In our practice, we have identified 2 types of betrayals that affect a relationship. The one that is most common revolves around sexual deviance and the other involves an emotional bond. We have been seeing more couples who explain that they had no intentions of betraying their spouse, however, their sexual desires grew and over powered them. Some have explained that the "cheating" started online where texting and emails were the easiest ways to express themselves and "one thing led to another."

Electronic conversations are becoming more and more prevalent as people don't see the need to call anyone and can easily express themselves through chat rooms, emails and texting. This opens the door to allow the development of a "soul tie."

I have seen couples who are very strong in their relationship allow themselves to get caught up in a relationship that leads to cheating. Once it starts, excuses are developed to justify everything that is done. The wrong suddenly looks okay although deep in the heart, the individual is aware that it isn't.

Some have shared that they were able to go from one partner to another for a long time without giving any clues to their spouses. However, this cannot go on forever. Someone will eventually find out. People set themselves up for great falls without thinking of all they can lose from giving in to what the flesh craves.

Affairs can start out as simple as going with a colleague during a lunch break or walking outside with a colleague. As a general rule, if I cannot do something in front of my spouse, then it's not worth doing it behind her back. Even when you've done nothing wrong technically, it could get you into trouble. Imagine someone calling your spouse and saying, "Hi Mary, I saw your husband with a woman walking in the mall." This person has no clue that it's your colleague, no clue it might be work related. Mary now becomes suspicious and furious, and her trust level starts to drop. Depending on the person, this might be addressed and if it is, Mary's spouse now starts questioning why he is being watched and why his wife does not trust him. An innocent situation has now reached the point of causing friction in the relationship.

Open communication between couples is key. You can never communicate enough. Showing that there are no hidden agendas will prevent your spouse from thinking negative thoughts about you.

In this case, the husband becomes frustrated and feels that he is under the radar, which opens the door for him to explore others. Some girl comes along and during his state of vulnerability, he caves in. All of this could have been avoided if he had informed his wife about this while he was at the shopping mall with the colleague from work.

A rule of thumb is to never be alone with another person of the opposite sex when married. It brings about several unanswered questions since people have no clue what type of relationship you have with that person. We need to stay away from the very appearance of evil.

The more we allow ourselves, to spend time with others alone, the greater the chances for a love relationship to develop. You might have watched the movie *Beauty and the Beast* or *King Kong*. Both movies clearly show how love has no boundaries. They are parallels of the nature of love between humans. If an "animal" or "beast" can win the love of someone of beauty, how much more can the average person easily become attached to someone? After all beauty is not necessarily what we see in the physical, but also the heart.

So what are some signs one can look for regarding infidelity? This was a question asked by one of my clients as she shared her heart regarding a suspicion that her husband, with whom she had been married with for 15 years, was cheating. She believed that he went on vacation to his homeland and met an old girlfriend. She found that her husband was "acting different" and was not sure what happened. She could recall that the changes took place after he came back from his vacation.

The client reported that she noticed her spouse appeared to be more distant. He seemed "cold." We explored the possibility that there was a change with his job, finances, family issues, parenting or health before assuming another person was in the picture. When this is your situation, before jumping to conclusions, it is best to share your heart and ask your spouse to explain what is on their mind.

Another issue that was brought up was the fact that this client's spouse would "snap" or become agitated very quickly for no apparent reason. When a person has a guilty conscience they can become defensive, therefore, when you notice your spouse "snaps" or become agitated for no apparent reason and it's not the norm, it should be taken into consideration. We inquired as to whether the client's spouse became upset when the client spoke about past girlfriends or tried to be direct on the subject of cheating. When a person is questioned as to their whereabouts it seems weird especially if this not something commonly practiced in the relationship.

The client shared about another observation she found strange, which was the fact that her spouse was becoming secretive about his cell phone, computer and emails. Her spouse had changed his password to all his electronic gadgets. Before, he would have his phone lying around but now it was always with him. His computer would be on most of the time before and now it was always off or he was logged off. It appeared that my client's spouse was hiding something.

Along with these other observations, there were a lot of excuses. My client's spouse no longer wanted to spend time with the extended family or his own children. He would work long hours and advised that he was too tired to go anywhere. The excuses became habitual and it became evident that there was something going on.

Another observation was a change of appearance. The client's spouse appeared to be regressing instead or adapting to his age. He looked like a teenager in his hairstyle and clothes. It was as though he wanted to impress someone new. He started to wear a new fragrance and shave more often than usual. His eating habits changed to reflect much healthier meal choices.

My client explained that she noticed that her spouse kept saying, "We need to spend more time with others." This is a clear sign that there are changes in one's life and you might need to boost up the relationship. If you notice this, join your spouse and make an effort to spend time together. The fact that you should know your spouse's likes and dislikes very well should be used to your advantage.

If your spouse has had a history of cheating, it will only heighten the chances that he will cheat again. The goal is allow your spouse to express how he or she feels with the assurance that you will not get upset. This is where the power to agree to disagree comes in handy. If cheating is a form of venting, then become the sponge to soak up the troubled heart. If it's a habit or behaviour then serious counselling is required. Fighting fire with fire is not the solution.

There is a saying that there is light at the end of every tunnel and I believe this for every issue in a relationship especially infidelity. The key is to keep working on the issue until the light overtakes the darkness.

In the case I referred to, one thing I noticed was the fact that the spouse showed deep remorse and the guilt was showed from the inside rather than material gifts or empty words. Instead of being angry, nasty and raging, this client's spouse expressed his feelings of shame and hurt.

The bonds of trust, the feeling of betrayal, the low self-esteem and the hurt that can stem from love affairs all can have a devastating effect on a relationship that often takes a serious intervention to mend. Add to this the deep feelings of shame that most people who engage in love affairs feel and the importance of avoiding them at all costs becomes clear.

Time is one of life's best medicines. It can bring about permanent healing and in a situation like this, we promote the allowance of time to take its course. Once both individuals agree to allow some time, we put effort into working on this issue without pointing fingers. The healing process will start and continue from there.

Kathleen and I are supporting more couples today who are dealing affairs than in the past. We have individuals in the marriage who explain that their intentions to have an affair were never there, until they felt there was no "life in the marriage." The romance faded, their lifestyle became too familiar and they could predict their day with each other. When there is nothing to stimulate the emotions, the desire grows to have the "forbidden fruit."

Getting older does not help, especially when you're hitting the midlife crisis. The feeling of losing your youth can be difficult for some, especially when your body fails to cooperate with the mind. Support one another as you go through this stage of life and draw even closer to one another to avoid the thought of feeling old.

Many men have affairs or fall into the trap of sexual adventures after their spouses give birth to a child. A man might take many cold showers, however, if there are no changes in the relationship he becomes vulnerable and can easily fall into the trap of an affair. No one should subject themselves or their partner to a sexless life. It will only create a separation in the relationship.

It must be said that the more you resist temptation, the easier it gets to resist temptation. It can be a struggle, but learn to say "no."

Keep the love fresh, fulfill the mission to stay together forever until death parts you and focus on solutions for marital issues.

Loving the person you chose to be your partner, your mate, your lover, your best friend, your companion and your spouse takes a great deal of investment. No relationship will survive with just 2 people living together. Time, money and effort need to be invested to see fruitfulness and happiness.

Points to Ponder:

1. What are the 2 types of betrayals that affect a relationship?
2. How does "open" communication close the doors to potential acts of infidelity?
3. Is this the first time you have heard of emotional infidelity? How easy is it to fall into its trap?
4. What happens when you continually resist temptation?

THE ART OF ROMANCE

Romance is an important part of a healthy relationship. Romance stimulates new areas in the emotional world whereas the satisfaction brought on by sex, which is also important, reaches a peak. Romance and sex work together hand-in-hand to bring the emotions alive in a relationship. When they are well-developed, love grows even stronger.

Romance is an art. My art teacher once told me, "Creating a good piece of art takes time." Romance is the same. Romance entails 2 artists working together over time on a masterpiece called a "relationship." It takes an artful skill to achieve a romantic moment.

> *Romance is an art whose masterpiece can become priceless depending on the time that is put into it.*

I remember our first dinner on a boat for our first anniversary. It was a surprise for Kathleen and I wanted to make the day special. Kathleen wowed me by the way she dressed. She wore a red dress, which brought out every feature of her body shape. It was amazing to think she had dressed up like this just for me. She wore a fragrance called "Anais, Anais" that carried a very subtle scent of a sweet flower. She wore red lipstick and looked stunning. Her red shoes, nylons and red purse were coordinated to perfection. She wore make-up that looked natural and sufficient jewellery that was not overbearing. Everything worked together just right to enhance her beauty.

Sitting and watching this beautiful woman placed a permanent smile on my face. I said to myself, *"Harrison, you did well for yourself. You married the world's most beautiful woman."* Her heart was like a diamond—precious and rare—and her attire was most befitting.

As I looked at Kathleen next to my side in that moment, holding her in my arms, kissing her beautiful lips and embracing her beauty, I realized that our piece of art had started. That day, the concept of family began in my heart.

Kathleen will tell you that up to this day when I think back on that evening, there's still a big smile on my face and nothing has been able to take it away. I consciously ask myself from time to time, *"What did I do to deserve this beautiful woman?"*

To create an atmosphere of romance, I encourage couples to groom themselves and look good for their spouse or partner especially on special nights out.

Another part of romance is learning how to master kisses and touch. Both kisses and touch are important components of romance. All men need to learn this concept if they want a healthy, long-lasting relationship.

Take charge in a subtle way by touching a woman softly with your fingers barely touching her skin. If you are in the process of creating a masterpiece, you will learn to hear the sounds a woman makes as you brush her hair back from her face, move her closer to your chest and hold her face lightly in your fingers as you kiss her. Passionately, you deepen the kiss and listen to her to understand what your next move is. You make her feel like she is the best thing that has happened to you and you cherish every moment. Your actions flow with her sound cues as she leads and you follow with the power of passion. You smell her body fragrance as you kiss her on the neck. You feel her body heat mixing with yours and respond accordingly. When all within you is crying out to be one with her, don't give in just yet; keep the momentum going as you keep working on the masterpiece. In this manner, you can create a piece of art by interacting with and responding to one another.

Love in the true sense is described in 1 Corinthians 3 of the Bible. As it suggests:

Some might believe that they have tongues like angels or they can speak like great politicians or can understand all mysteries and all knowledge or have unmatched faith. However, if they cannot love or show love this has no value. Some feel that if they give away all their possessions and hand over their bodies to torture they may boast, but if love is not present that individual has gained nothing.

Love is patient. Love is kind. Love is not envious or boastful or arrogant or rude. It does not insist on its own way. It is not irritable or resentful. It does not rejoice in wrongdoing, but rejoices in the truth. It bears all things, believes all things, hopes all things, and endures all things. Love never ends.

With this in mind, remember that when love in this true sense is absent, the art of romance will not come to its fullness.

Romance is an art whose masterpiece can become priceless depending on the time that is put into it. The more time invested, the more value it will hold. Men need to become progressive in developing creative ideas to surprise their spouses without looking for anything in return. Some ideas we suggest to couples are as follows.

- Try doing something small that your spouse usually does. You're in the kitchen and your spouse s in the living room. The doorbell rings. Instead of yelling, "Get the doorbell!" stop what you're doing, pass her in the living room and get the doorbell. When there's a piece of paper lying on the floor and your spouse is typically the one to pick it up, instead of ignoring it, you pick it up.
- Change from your work clothes to something more pleasant for your spouse.
- Wear a nice fragrance.
- Try purchasing a little gift now and again.
- Write a love note.
- From the time we started to notice girls we learned the concept of writing poems as a means of expressing our affections. Writing a poem is an easy and meaningful way to create romance when it comes from the heart.
- Sometimes Kathleen will make us a nice hot bath with candles, bubbles, sweet fragrance, soft music and a cold

drink. The atmosphere alone takes away the heaviness of a bad day. Sometimes I do the same for her. What makes the scene complete is having her with me in the bath. The conversation can last for hours as we talk about each other, the children, future plans and so on.

- Blindfold your spouse and have them guess what you are doing. For those who are married, you can slowly undress each other and using a feather, slowly stroke each other's body. (Some people like the unknown or the unpredictable.)

- On your way home from work, stop off at the coffee shop and invest a few dollars on a coffee and a treat: maybe your spouse's favourite chocolate, candy or fruit.

- Think of a quick dinner and let your spouse know you have a surprise so she does not have to cook. Bring home a take-out meal and light some candles to make the evening romantic. Cooking a romantic dinner would be even better. This is a common one. To spruce it up further, play some favourite love songs. In fact, every couple should have "their song," a love song that is special to the 2 of them.

- Create a collection of sayings or a scrapbook that reminds you of your spouse. Creating memories with your spouse or partner is very important. It's like stamping the brain with an imprint that keeps the memories alive. Sometimes reading cards you wrote to each other, letters or poems is nice. Some have gathered items for years and placed them in a box or album and use this as a time capsule for emotionally rainy days.

- Learning to declare love publicly can be challenging, especially in some cultures. I know in my culture you do not see many couples holding hands, hugging each other or kissing in public. I was always asked to kiss Kathleen or hold her hands when were newlyweds by her family members, especially when it came to photos. I would turn red (no one saw but I knew I did). It eventually became natural, and was especially comforting when we went through difficult times in our lives such as the death of our close friend. We no longer take a second thought about publicly declaring our love, as it comes naturally.

- Learning to feed each other can be romantic. It depends on the type of food and where you do it. Most people like the grape concept or strawberries with whipped cream. It all depends on what you like and what your spouse enjoys. I enjoy chocolate, raspberries and peanuts.
- Some women are attracted to a tool belt and seeing their spouse doing some work around the house creates an atmosphere of romance. Perhaps you might learn how to become handier around the house.
- One item on my list that is very common when I ask couples to do homework is the full-body massage. Most couples enjoy massages. I have suggested getting a hotel and taking some time away from everyone. Carry a shower curtain or something that is soft to a hotel with your spouse and spread it over the bed. Then use baby oil and massage each other. It feels sensational.
- Plan a trip to the movies and instead of getting all caught up in the movie, make out like teenagers. The more you make an effort to show love, the more love gets awakened.
- Be creative with picnics in the woods or park. Sometimes we are too cheap to invest in one another and buying dinner or going out to an expensive restaurant becomes an issue. A picnic is one cheaper way to be creative and romantic at the same time. Besides, simple is good at times.
- Learn how to kiss in the rain, in the park, at the door, at dinner, in the car, at the shopping mall or on a walk. Learn how to kiss and kiss and kiss some more. Song of Songs 1:2 in the Bible says, "Let him kiss me with the kisses of his mouth. For your love is better than wine." If kissing was not important, God would not have recorded it in, arguably, the most romantic book of the Bible. And remember, a perfunctory peck on the cheek does not generate the full power of a kiss. A peck is the same type of kiss you would give to your grandmother, parents or friends. I remind Kathleen that I don't want the "grandma's kiss" when I am rushing out the door.
- Some guys might need to study up on how to keep the "first date" special. Show up at the door of her home with a bunch

of roses, dress up, smell good and prepare a clean car. Recreating the first date in a mature relationship can bring old feelings alive and keep the love growing.

- Cooking together is a good idea as well.
- Socializing with other couples or groups can also create romance. It will enlarge your sphere of appreciation as you will always find that you have something special together compared to the other couples you are with. A whisper or a touch of your spouse during your time out can only add to the art being created. Kathleen once told me that putting my arms around her in the public still gives her the shivers.

The movies, books and magazines often portray perfect images of relationships. Kathleen and I are hoping for a new breed of couples to rise up and maintain a level of relationships the world has never seen before. One that joins hearts and souls with a love the movies can't even dream about. I believe romance will have an important part to play in the realization of this hope.

Points to Ponder:

1. Romance is an art that takes 2 individuals in a relationship to create. What have you created together with your spouse that you can call a piece of art?
2. What are some romantic suggestions besides cooking dinner for each other?
3. Why is romance not considered an important entity in most relationships that are over 5 years old?

GOAL DIGGER

Clarifying and articulating goals is an indispensable skill for success in any relationship. A goal-setter is someone who, of the top of their head, identifies goals and tries to achieve them. A "goal digger" digs deeper to find goals that are thoughtful and tangible and endures a process with family and mentors to shape and achieve their goals.

While some couples might be well-versed goal diggers, the majority of couples are not. Most couples have an overall idea of what they want to achieve, however, the persistency to stay focused becomes difficult when goals are not broken down into specific, practical actions that can be taken.

> *Most couples have an overall idea of what they want to achieve, however, the persistency to stay focused becomes difficult when goals are not broken down into specific, practical actions that can be taken.*

Kathleen and I have learned the importance of setting goals in order for us to move ahead as individuals, as a couple and a family. We move from having that initial thought of what we would like to see in our lives to making it a reality by applying some practical principles.

The key step for each goal digger is to go ahead and start planning. Goals might not be fully developed as a result of this stage, however, taking some time to ponder goals can help to set the foundation that will clarify the goals better down the line.

When goals are not achieved it brings about a stunted growth in the relationship as couples don't have much to look forward to. The achievement of goals is a source of confidence that is good for the relationship. Not having goals keeps us living like a fish in a bowl rather than a fish in an ocean.

Kathleen and I have found that couples who lack goals in their relationship focus on themselves. They look at what they can get out of a relationship instead of what they should be giving into the relationship. As goals are set, couples will assist each other and the end result is the goals take on a less self-centred nature.

As in the principle of synergy, as couples assist each other and work together, they are far more successful than if they were approaching their goals as 2 separate individuals.

We encourage couples to set future-oriented goals. The thought that we are building a future together as a couple and focusing on a future of success, will encourage our hearts to stay persistent.

Couples need to be realistic when setting goals. They need to consider whether or not the goals are attainable so they do not end up getting frustrated during the stage of working towards their goals.

Goals can involve any area of our life, such as our education, family, career, friends, vacations, hobbies or spirituality (e.g., finding a good church). There are a number of traits that a good and achievable goal possesses. Good goals are well-defined and specific. We like to use SMART goals as our template to establish our goals. SMART goals are *specific*, *measurable*, *action-oriented*, *realistic*, and *timely*. With these qualities in mind, we are able to reach greater accomplishments and in a shorter time frame.

Being goal diggers has enabled Kathleen and me to achieve a number of dreams despite very busy schedules. Kathleen went back to school when we were newlyweds. She graduated carrying our first child at 7 months pregnant. She worked and I went to school and we coordinated our time to care for our baby. We travelled, did missions work and raised our family. We lived in a war-torn country with 4 children and continued with the goals we set for our lives. Yes, it was difficult and there were days when I was overwhelmed. I remember crying as I studied late hours or those rough days when I would fall asleep at my job. However, the goals we set kept us moving ahead.

In our house, we set our goals at the start of each year and as a family we fast for 21 days on the 'Daniel Fast," where we pray for each other's goals and the family goals. Our miracle goals are the ones we keep especially close to heart. (Miracle goals are ones that might appear to be impossible but yet deep down in your heart you know that there is a possibility they can be achieved.)

We exam our lives and discuss the dreams and whether or not they are realistic. The family discussion gives others the opportunity to assist with their personal contacts or offer up suggestions, recommendations, prayers and encouragement.

Working together with your spouse and the rest of your family helps a great deal. You become accountable to others for your goals and are more likely to be committed to them when others are involved. Remember, your spouse should be your number one fan.

We have found prayer to be instrumental in helping us to meet our goals. A prime example was my goal to change my employment hours from 12-hour days to 8-hour days. Kathleen and I felt we needed to spend more time with our children and keep our weekends open to develop spirituality in the home. The entire family prayed and we saw God open the doors for me to do this. It was an easy transition and the goal was met.

Doubts can assail you from all sides. They can come from people you least expect. There might be thoughts revolving in your mind that you are wasting time. One suggestion that helps is to develop a reward system to treat yourself whenever you achieve your goals. You can even celebrate the accomplishment of certain steps along the way towards your goal. Celebrate each milestone you accomplish and share it with those who care about you.

Kathleen and I have learned that there is a need for feedback when pursuing goals. We have not met anyone who has all the answers to life's questions, but we have found another person can give helpful feedback. Dr. Randy Neilson and Jill Neilson have been mentors in our lives along with some others we consider dear to us. Kathleen and I have learned from our mentors that goals often need to be adjusted, reassessed and redirected. Second opinions are very important since sometimes we can get stuck with conflicting perspectives that can become obstacles.

Kathleen and I had known the Neilson's for over 15 years when we found out that they had moved to a nearby city and were pastoring at a local church: Bramalea Christian Fellowship Church. As we reacquainted ourselves, we soon realized that we had similar spiritual DNA. They became our mentors and poured valuable insight into our lives, shaping a lot of the goals we have set.

I remember the day we were having coffee and Dr. Neilson advised that success is "not about quantity but quality," adding, "It's about triumphing over your adversaries, barriers and the negative words people say to stop you." Dr. Neilson explained the concept of prioritizing individual, couple and family goals.

Once, Dr. Neilson and Jill advised Kathleen and me that we "let go and let God," which I thought we were already doing. I assumed that by becoming busy doing all that we thought we should be doing we were aligning ourselves with God's will. However, it was time for Kathleen and me to get out of life's whirlwind and move on to more strategic goals that aligned with God's divine plan, purpose and destiny for our lives.

That day Kathleen and I went home and we looked at all we had accomplished together as a couple and, upon reflection, I could feel joy rising up inside of me. We then prioritized our new goals and looked at what was most important.

I completed my PhD, resigned from running the college and 2 casual jobs. We refocused on family time, nourishing Kathleen's goals, focusing my career and building our spiritual foundation.

I must say, I felt it was a lot to give up and I initially had a feeling of letting myself down. It took a few weeks to swallow what Randy and Jill advised and adjust to our new decisions, as it meant making changes to our life in areas that we felt were accomplishments. Despite our reservations we pondered on the words said and took them to heart and they had a great impact on our relationship and family life.

Points to Ponder:

1. Why is it important to set goals with your spouse?
2. What's the difference between a goal-setter and a goal digger?
3. Name some "miracle goals" and "tangible goals" you have set together.
4. Who is investing into your life? Are you allowing others in authority to speak into your life even if it hurts and involves you making changes?

WE CAN WORK IT OUT

It has been said that the basis for any relationship is sincere communication and faith. It has been proven that lack of effective communication creates dead air in a relationship causing it to be stifled. It takes 2 people to create a spark in a relationship just like 2 rocks that rub against each other can create a spark.

I believe a life of breakups is a choice we all have the ability to make. Getting into a relationship is easy. Maintaining and upholding one can be difficult. However, with the right effort, a healthy relationship is possible. It requires the acquisition of skills and education just like applying for a new job, but it is attainable. Relationships play an important role in our lives. People who live alone might struggle and maintain a distant relationship with friends and family. Thus, a healthy relationship with a spouse is well worth pursuing.

> *I believe a life of breakups is a choice we all have the ability to make.*

I had a close friend who shared his story with me which is a great example of the power of forgiveness. My friend and his spouse had a relationship that revolved around his lies and deception. My friend had another life that was kept secret for many years. This man had several women in his life. He had sex with his sister-in-law, his close friend's wife, his colleagues at work, the next-door neighbour, his bank teller, the grocery store cashier, the hotel receptionist and others he could not recall when sharing his story.

My friend had explained he started to be sexually promiscuous when he was about 14 years old. He visited his next-door neighbour and they were playing together. They started to explore each other and he ended up having sex with her and her sister. All through high school he struggled with sex. He slept with as many women as he could and on one occasion with his school teacher.

This friend got involved with abusing street drugs and at times sold his body to both men and women for drugs. He abused every illegal drug on the market and when he could not find drugs, he used alcohol. He lived away from his family and no one knew he was living this lifestyle. He only called his parents when he was sober or needed money.

I came into this friend's life when he was on the verge of suicide. He attempted to overdose on medications and alcohol. He was taken to the hospital where he was cared for. I assisted with connecting him to community support. He cleaned himself up, went through rehabilitation and became a totally new person. However, the biggest issue he still had to deal with was his addiction to sex.

We spent sufficient time together where I became his "accountable friend." About a year a half later he met a beautiful girl who practically fell into his arms and they were crazy in love with each other. She became aware of his past issues and she said, "We can work it out."

The day of the wedding came and my friend found himself having sex with his fiancé's best friend. It was neither a pleasant scene nor a situation I wanted to be part of. He was very apologetic and tried to make me promise that I would not expose his secret.

He said, "We can work this out," and I said "No." He was building a foundation of lies starting out his marriage like this. My friend explained that he had no intentions of sleeping with anyone, he was aware of his weakness and all the things he should have done to prevent being in a vulnerable situation.

He cried and showed every sign of being remorseful. He even had his fiancé's best friend explain to me how she had initiated the act. After 40 minutes of explanations, we all agreed that he should share with his fiancé what he and her best friend had done. This was a very awkward situation.

My friend sat with his bride-to-be and explained what he did. She was very angry and upset, screaming and yelling at him. They had a long discussion and he proposed the option of calling the wedding off and allowing some time to work on this problem.

My friend's fiancé knew his history and she became an asset in his life by forgiving him. He was soon able to refocus his frustrations and his ability to cope was based on having someone who believed in him. His fiancé made the choice to live with someone who she knew had a very difficult history instead of walk away. As they sat together and she asked herself all the questions as to why she should not be with my friend, she found more reasons as to why she should be with him.

There were a couple of good things going for this relationship. Both of them were young Christians and they had several people in their life who believed in them. My friend was accountable to the right mentors and support systems to which he was responsive.

They were married and were happy together until death separated them. My friend told me on several occasions that when his wife said, "We can work this out," the words were like acid that killed his sexual addictions.

My friend died in my arms from an illness that was difficult to treat. He died knowing there was someone there who chose to love him through the thick and thin. If there were a perfect example of true love to share, it is this one. In this case, love was not ruled by the weaknesses present but was found in the solution, "We can work it out."

Points to Ponder:

1. What are some reasons as to why couples might feel they cannot work out their issues in a relationship?
2. What are some proven tips to work on relationship issues?
3. Why do couples come to a point of believing they are unable to work out their issues?
4. When is a good time to work on issues?

CONCLUSION

There are issues in every relationship. These can develop into even bigger problems and can completely destroy relationships when they are not addressed in a timely manner. Issues are like little sparks that can get out of control and become a raging fire. They start out as small signs of the presence of a problem which are often not taken seriously. Like a fire quickly becomes kindled, the issues can quickly bring a couple to the point of separation or divorce.

I see breakups to be one of the leading causes of depression and emotional wounds in society. With the amount of breakups we are seeing today, this is an issue that must be addressed with a sense of urgency. Sometimes it appears that people prefer to breakup and live a lonely life rather than to work on their unhealthy relationships. If a person is not well physically, we quickly seek medical support. How about when a couple has an unhealthy relationship? There should be that same drive to seek out psychological support.

Spiritual beliefs and faith play an important part in every relationship. They keep godly morals present in the life of a couple. A covenant is sealed by God and no man can break it. Without good morals and faith, couples have no rules to follow except, "Whatever feels good, do it." With God in the picture there is an obligation to live righteous lives. Whether you are a believer or not, every couple should have their spiritual life examined. Spirituality has been proven to keep morals in the relationship. It has given strength to those on the verge of separation or divorce. And we have found that a couple who prays together really does stay together.

Every couple will have its own culture, rituals and traditions. Kathleen and I have developed our own. One of the things we do, for instance, is have coffee together in the early morning. You might do something completely different. Then there are the things that tend to work for every relationship, many of which have been suggested in this book. Being in the habit of kissing is a perfect example. A kiss goodbye gives your spouse an assurance that you are taking their heart with you until you see them again. I trust that these and the other suggestions presented in this book will help you to kiss *breakups* goodbye forever.